T5-AEY-769

THE PAPACY AND THE KINGDOM OF ITALY

THE PAPACY AND THE KINGDOM OF ITALY

BY

HUMPHREY JOHNSON, M.A.
AUTHOR OF "ANTHROPOLOGY AND THE FALL"

LONDON
SHEED AND WARD
31 PATERNOSTER ROW, E.C.
1926

WITH the exception of a small number of passages this work has appeared in serial form in the *Catholic Gazette*.

Made and Printed in Great Britain at
The Mayflower Press, Plymouth. William Brendon & Son, Ltd.

CONTENTS

CHAPTER I

CAVOUR'S CONFLICT WITH THE CHURCH

THE transference of the seat of imperial government from the Tiber to the Bosphorus early in the fourth century is an event which, according to our inclinations, we shall interpret as a peculiar disposition of Divine Providence for releasing the bishops of Rome from the imminent menace of secular interference in the discharge of their world-wide apostolate, or as a fortuitous occurrence which enabled the spiritual overseers of the former capital of the world to masquerade in the now unwanted trappings of the pagan emperors and to transform the religion of the Sermon on the Mount into the most perfectly organised system of sacerdotal imposture that mankind has ever seen. Whatever be our view, we find that at the beginning of the eighth century, the Senate being now extinct, the popes are the virtual rulers of the ancient "duchy" of Rome or Patrimony of St. Peter. A few years later Lombard pressure, which has overthrown the Byzantine exarchate of Ravenna, compels the Pope, no longer trusting in the Cæsar upon the Golden Horn, to seek an ally beyond the Alps, in the person of Pepin the Short. In consequence of this "the Frank bestowed on the papal chair all that belonged to the exarchate in North Italy, receiving as the meed of his services the title of Patrician." (Bryce, *The Holy Roman Empire*, 4th Edition, 1892, 40.)

At a later date the bequests of the great Countess of Tuscany augment the possessions of the Roman Church, and Innocent III strengthens the papal hold upon Umbria by acquiring Spoleto, thus creating a bridge between the "Patrimonium" and the Adriatic coast.[1] The residence of the popes at Avignon (1309–1376) weakened their authority over their Italian possessions, and Innocent VI (1352–1362), after the failure of Rienzi's attempt to revive the Roman Republic, sent the Spanish Cardinal Albornoz as his Vicar-General to restore papal authority over the communes of Central Italy. A century and a half, however, was to elapse till the campaigns of Julius II (1503–1513), by recovering Bologna and Perugia for the Church and expelling the Venetians from the Pentapolis, firmly established papal rule over that compact block of territory, extending from Terracina to the valley of the

[1] In 1201 Otho IV recognised as Papal territory "*tota terra quae est a Radicofano usque Ceperanum ; exarchatus Ravennae, Pentapolis, Marchiae, Ducatus Spoletanus, terrae comitissae Mathildis, comitatus Brittennorii cum aliis adjacentibus terris expressio in multis privilegiis imperatorum a tempore Lodoicii.*" (*Rambler*, March 1860, 313, note.)

Po, which was known in modern times as the States of the Church. Julius also added to the pontifical dominions Parma and Piacenza, which had formerly belonged to the duchy of Milan. Paul III constituted this territory into a duchy, which he bestowed on his son Pierluigi Farnese in 1545. On the extinction of the legitimate Este line in 1597, Clement VIII established his claim to the old papal fief of Ferrara;[1] and the extinction of the della Rovere line brought about the reversion of Urbino to Urban VIII in 1631.[2] This was the last addition made to the papal territories.

In addition to the "Patrimonium," Umbria and the Marches in Central, and the Romagna in Northern Italy, the popes possessed the enclaves of Benevento and Pontecorvo in Neapolitan territory, and that of Avignon and the Comtat-Venaissin in France.

There have been minds in all ages to whom the question has presented itself, whether rule over these wide dominions could be fittingly combined with the office of one who claimed to be the Vicar of Him who had not where to lay His head. A moment's reflection should, however, suffice to convince us that the negative answer to this question is the more superficial one. Sovereignty over Rome and its adjacent territory, whatever its later disadvantages, was clearly the only means of

[1] Ranke, *History of the Popes* (Bohn's Popular Library), ii, 74–83.
[2] *Ib.*, 325–331.

preserving the spiritual independence of the Pope in late mediæval and even in early modern times. Yet it had its dangers as well as its advantages. As a temporal prince, the Pope had no overlord who could coerce him, yet he was also, like other temporal princes, liable to witness a hostile invasion of his territory. So long as Europe was Catholic the religious veneration with which the successor of Peter was regarded, though it could not avert such episodes as the tragedy at "Alagna," in which Dante saw the vinegar and the gall "renewed,"[1] did at least provide the Pope with some measure of security against violence. The Reformation did not immediately make a substantial change in this situation. There were indeed many Lutherans in the army of the Constable of Bourbon, which sacked Rome in 1527, but they were in the service of a Catholic monarch, and no Protestant State was sufficiently near to the Holy City to be able to employ violence against the head of the Catholic religion. For a moment there was, indeed, a threat of danger from another quarter. The power of the Turk reached its zenith in the long reign of Suleiman the Magnificent (1520–1566) and the menace of a Moslem invasion of Italy loomed upon the horizon. The victory of Lepanto (1571) dispelled this sinister possibility, and no non-Catholic State was allowed by geography again to threaten Rome till the Treaty of Utrecht

[1] *Purgatorio*, XX.

(1713) made Great Britain a Mediterranean Power by confirming her in possession of Gibraltar and Minorca. The peril which might arise to Rome from this source was noted by an English traveller in 1765. "Rome," he wrote, "has nothing to fear from the Catholic Powers, who respect it with a superstitious veneration as the metropolitan seat of their religion: but the popes will do well to avoid misunderstandings with the maritime Protestant states, especially the English, who, being masters of the Mediterranean and in possession of Minorca, have it in their power at all times to land a body of troops within four leagues of Rome, and to take the city without opposition." (Tobias Smollett, *Travels through France and Italy*, Letter XXX.) A few years earlier the contingency here envisaged seemed likely to materialise. Prince Charles Edward Stuart had sought asylum in Avignon, in consequence of the clause in the Treaty of Aix-la-Chapelle which required France to expel members of the exiled royal family of England; and a threatened bombardment of Civita Vecchia by the English fleet led Benedict XIV to request the prince to leave his territory. It is even related that the great Pope once humorously threatened to abolish Lent in order to cripple England by ruining her fishing trade.

Yet the temporal power was already beginning to crumble. In the war of the Austrian Succession the Pope could not prevent the violation of his territory by the rival armies; and the victory of Don Carlos of Bourbon over the Austrians at Velletri, which secured the independence of Southern Italy, was fought almost within sight of Rome. At the peace which concluded the war the Powers, moreover, disregarded the claims of the Pope to the reversion of Parma, upon the extinction of the Farnese line, Elizabeth Farnese, Queen of Philip V of Spain, securing the succession for her son. Troublous years followed the death of Benedict XIV (1758), and in the critical negotiations which preceded the suppression of the Society of Jesus (1773) Choiseul seized Avignon and Tanucci, Benevento and Pontecorvo, to put pressure upon the Pope.

Under the pontificate of Clement XIV's successor, Pius VI (1775–1799), there fell upon the temporal power of the Pope the first of those great blows under which it was finally to succumb, and no heretic Power delivered it, but the elder daughter of the Church herself. Revolutionary France entered Italy in 1796. Charles Emmanuel IV of Savoy saw his continental dominions fall into her hands, and took refuge in Sardinia under the protection of the English Fleet. First the Romagna was wrested from the Pope, and in 1798 General Berthier occupied the Eternal City and the Holy Father was carried away to die in exile. A few months after his death the Cardinals elected his successor in Venice. To Pius VII the motto of his predecessor, *Peregrinus Apostolicus*, rendered apt by his visit to Vienna and his death at Valence, might no less have applied. Twice he crossed the Alps, once to anoint an emperor and the second time as a prisoner.

On the collapse of the French Empire in 1814 the Papacy recovered its Italian possessions almost in their entirety, though Avignon was not restored to it. The Italian settlement which was reached at Vienna was, however, one which could be justified from the point of view neither of geography nor of language. The Venetian Republic was abolished in favour of Austria, who also recovered Milan. Venice's ancient rival Genoa was given to Piedmont to strengthen it as a bulwark against France. The Bourbons were restored to the throne of the Two Sicilies and also eventually in 1847 to the duchy of Parma, on the death of the Empress Marie Louise, to whom it had been assigned for life. The grand-duchy of Tuscany and the duchy of Modena ruled by Austrian archdukes were, of course, but satellite states of the Hapsburg Empire. Of the Italian islands, Sardinia was retained by the House of Savoy and continued to give it its regal title;[1] Corsica was

[1] The House of Savoy traces its descent from Humbert of the White Hand (*Biancamano*), Count of Savoy (died 1048). A member of the family was Archbishop of Canterbury in the reign of Henry III and another built the old Savoy Palace. Count Amadeus VIII was created duke by the Emperor Sigismund in 1416. Although a layman, he was elected Pope by the schismatic Council of Basle in 1439, and styled himself Felix V. He subsequently submitted to Nicholas V,

retained by France, and Malta and Gozo by England.

The restored rulers seemed anxious to forget that the French Revolution had ever occurred, and proceeded to govern their subjects upon this assumption. A strong demand for national unity and constitutionalist, as opposed to absolutist, government arose as a protest against this artificial division of Italy, and against the despotic methods of the restored rulers. With regard to the manner in which the unification of the peninsula was to be accomplished, there existed two schools of thought. The more conservative one, whose principal luminaries were Rosmini, Gioberti, and Cesare Balbo, first constitutional prime minister of Piedmont, taking account of the divergent traditions of the different provinces, looked forward to a unification of Italy upon federal lines. The other and more radical one desired a more complete unity under a central government, which should be either republican, or monarchical, under the House of Savoy. On the supposition of a federal Italy, its only possible president was the Pope; since he was the only Italian sovereign towards

who created him Cardinal of Santa Sabina. Felix V was the last anti-Pope. Victor Amadeus II (1675–1730) entered the war of the Spanish succession on the side of France, but went over to the Austrians during the course of the struggle. For his services to the Emperor he was created King of Sicily at the peace of Utrecht, a title which he exchanged in 1720 for that of King of Sardinia. Pope Clement XI, regarding both islands as papal fiefs, made an ineffectual protest against a treaty which disposed of them without regard to his rights.

whom the others could cherish no sense of dynastic rivalry.

Attached to the national movement was an anti-religious one, whose partisans desired the overthrow of the old order of things, because of the Catholic character of the institutions and laws with which it was so closely bound up.

Of all the Italian States Piedmont was the one in which Liberalism of the continental type had made the greatest headway ; and to it the revolutionaries of the others looked for support. They at first pinned their hopes upon Charles Albert, Prince of Carignano, who succeeded to the throne of Sardinia in 1831, on the death of his distant relative, Charles Felix, in whom the elder branch of the House of Savoy became extinct in the male line. Charles Albert had in his youth been on friendly terms with the Carbonari, if not actually, like Louis Napoleon, a member of their society. After his accession, however, his ardent Catholicism earned for him the hatred of the Radicals of Turin and of the Republicans of Genoa. When in 1848 the downfall of the Orléans monarchy kindled the flame of revolution throughout Europe, the King, who retained his passionate desire to free Italian soil from foreign domination, undertook two campaigns against Austria, in 1848 and 1849, to accomplish this purpose. Abdicating after his defeat at Novara by Radetzky, he retired to a monastery at Oporto, where he died, and Italy, except Piedmont, settled down to ten years of political reaction. The Pope, the King of Naples, and the Grand Duke of Tuscany, who had quitted their capitals during the revolutionary ferment, upon their restoration exhibited but little faith in parliamentary institutions. Charles Albert's eldest son, Victor Emmanuel II, threw in his lot with the Liberals from the outset of his reign. Their first measure for weakening the influence of the Church in Piedmont was a Bill for abolishing her right of jurisdiction over clerics, together with the right of asylum and certain feast days. Its author was Count Siccardi, Minister of Justice in D'Azeglio's Cabinet. The privileges which it attacked were secured by Concordat and the Pope refused to yield with regard to them. It was submitted to the Sub-Alpine Parliament in 1850 and passed the Chamber by 107 votes to 42, and the Senate by 52 votes to 29.[1] The Catholic party placed their last hope of defeating the measure in the royal veto. The King was entreated by his wife and mother not to assent to a measure which violated solemn engagements contracted by his house towards the Holy See. He yielded, however, to the Liberal pressure, and the Bill became law. The Archbishops of Turin and Cagliari felt it their duty to resist it, and in consequence suffered arrest and banishment. The refusal of the Last Sacraments, upon his death-bed, to Cavaliere di Santa Rosa, Minister of Commerce and Agriculture, because

[1] Cappelletti, *Storia d'Italia* (1915), ii, 354.

he refused to sign a recantation of the part which he had taken in passing the law, led to violent reprisals on the part of the Government and of the Liberal mob of Turin.

Shortly afterwards followed the introduction of civil marriage. There was no national demand for this measure, whose avowed object was to weaken the influence of the Church in family life in a country hitherto noted for its profoundly Catholic sentiments. The controversy which it stirred up led to the resignation of D'Azeglio; after which Cavour became President of the Council. Next came the inevitable attack on the religious orders. In November, 1854, Urbano Rattazzi, in his capacity of Minister of the Interior, laid before Parliament a measure for the suppression of all "useless" religious corporations. The motives which inspired the measure were the same as those which had inspired Henry VIII. The Liberals believed that, once the orders had been dissolved, it would be a comparatively light task to reduce the secular clergy to a state of subservience to the Government. The ostensible object of the measure was to relieve the strain upon the Treasury. Towards the end of the year the King wrote to the Premier, La Marmora, that his wife and his mother told him that he was killing them. Their words came true with unexpected suddenness. On January 12th, 1855, the Queen-Dowager died, and a week later the Queen, Marie-Adelaide of Austria, died in child-bed.

Three weeks later the King also lost his only brother, the Duke of Genoa. These lugubrious events created a profound impression in the little kingdom, and pious minds saw in them a warning sent by God to Victor Emmanuel to sever his alliance with the enemies of the Church. The King himself seems also for a moment to have regarded them in that light. Taking advantage of his scruples in the matter of the Religious Orders Bill, the Piedmontese Bishops offered to pay 900,000 lire into the Treasury if the measure were withdrawn. This proposal was made on their behalf in the Senate by Mgr. Calabianca,[1] Bishop of Casale Monferrato, later Archbishop of Milan, and patron during his youth of the present Pope. The episcopal offer was rejected and the real purpose of the Bill became revealed. It received the royal assent and became law on May 28th, 1855. On July 26th the Pope excommunicated all who were responsible for the anti-religious laws. Such was the religious situation in the state which was destined within a few years to conquer Italy.

"*Italia farà da se*" had been Charles Albert's motto, but Victor Emmanuel and Cavour were wiser, and knew that without the aid of foreign arms their country could not be freed from foreign rule. As the godson of Prince Camillo Borghese, brother-in-law of Napoleon I, Cavour's connection with the Bonaparte family dated

[1] Massari, *Il Conte di Cavour* (1873), 121.

back to the day when the Princess Pauline had held him at the font. To her nephew Napoleon III, desirous of enhancing the prestige of his throne by a victorious war, the Piedmontese statesman now turned. By his participation in the Crimean War he had had an opportunity, at the Congress at Paris, to bring the Italian question to the Emperor's notice. Yet Louis Napoleon's idea of a united Italy differed fundamentally from Cavour's. No good Frenchman could without misgivings view the possibility of the emergence of a new great Power in the Mediterranean. Yet the Emperor was not without sympathy for Italy, and desired to assist her towards the attainment of her unity, in such a manner, however, as not to injure France. Cavour visited him secretly at Plombières in July, 1858, and, as the imperial phaeton wended its way through the wooded valleys of the Vosges, the Emperor and he concocted a scheme for the establishment of an Italian federation. It was to consist of four states. Firstly, there was to be a kingdom of Upper Italy ruled over by Victor Emmanuel, which should include the Lombardo-Venetian provinces together with the Emilia (as the Romagna, Parma, and Modena were called). The Marches and Umbria, united to Tuscany, were to constitute a kingdom of Etruria. Napoleon seems at one time to have thought of placing the Bourbons of Parma upon its throne; his eventual candidate, however, was his cousin, Prince Napoleon Joseph, a man of disreputable life, whom Victor Emmanuel's elder daughter, the Princess Clothilde, a child of fifteen, was for dynastic reasons inveigled into marrying. Pius IX was to retain Rome; but for the loss of the greater part of his dominions he was to be compensated by becoming the titular president of the confederation. (Its real head was, of course, to be the Emperor of the French.) Finally, upon the throne of the Two Sicilies the Bourbons were to be replaced by Lucien Murat, King Joachim's second son. France was to receive Savoy and Nice, and an excuse was to be found for attacking Austria. In April, 1859, Austria, falling into a trap laid for her by Cavour, declared war against Piedmont, to whose assistance the Emperor of the French sent 200,000 men. After successes gained by the Piedmontese at Palestro and Montebello, the French victory at Magenta on June 4th enabled Napoleon III and Victor Emmanuel to enter Milan on the 8th amid scenes of delirious enthusiasm. Following upon a further defeat at Solferino, Austria yielded up Lombardy (except Mantua and Peschiera) to Piedmont. Napoleon, alarmed by the mobilisation of Prussia, feared to proceed to the liberation of Venetia.[1]

Meanwhile revolutions in Tuscany, Parma,

[1] The Emperor's conduct was probably also dictated by the growing alarm caused in French Catholic circles by the aggrandisement of Piedmont and by the unsatisfactory state of the health of the Army.

Modena, and the Romagna led to their incorporation into Piedmont (March, 1860). In May Garibaldi set sail from Quarto with a handful of volunteers to aid an insurrection against the Bourbons in Sicily. Overrunning the whole island, except the citadel of Messina, he crossed over to the mainland in August and advanced on Naples. The troops sent against him by the feeble Government of Francis II melted away as he approached, and the unfortunate King, surrounded by treachery, abandoned his capital and retired to the fortified peninsula of Gaeta. Garibaldi entered Naples in triumph, became Dictator, and advanced to the Volturno. But his popularity soon began to wane. Cavour was alarmed lest he should proclaim a republic and proceed to attack Rome, a step which must provoke the intervention of France. Meanwhile there were signs that a reaction in favour of the Bourbons might set in, while the Muratists were becoming active. Faced with this complex situation, Cavour executed the masterstroke which was to transform the kingdom of Sardinia into the kingdom of Italy. Piedmontese troops crossed the Pope's frontier at Cattolica, dispersed his army under Lamoricière at Castelfidardo on September 18th, and in October crossed the Neapolitan frontier. Victor Emmanuel himself now headed the invasion, and, advancing through the Abruzzi, grasped Garibaldi's hand at Teano.

This lawless aggression aroused a storm of

indignation throughout Europe, which found expression in the withdrawal of the diplomats from Turin. Only Sir James Hudson and the Swedish Minister remained at their posts.[1] Even the French Emperor, though secretly in collusion with the invaders, withdrew his representative. England, in the person of Lord John Russell, blessed the invasion of the Papal States.[2] The blessing which Sixtus V had bestowed on Medina Sidonia, when he sailed from Cadiz, was avenged. King Francis maintained his resistance, made memorable by the heroism of the Queen (who, it may be remembered, died only in 1925), till February 13th, 1861. The withdrawal of the French fleet then compelled him to capitulate. The Marches, Umbria, Naples, and Sicily were annexed by Victor Emmanuel, who was proclaimed King of Italy at Turin on March 14th, 1861.

Within less than three months of the conclusion of this great achievement Cavour, his constitution worn out by the strain of the preceding years, after having received absolution from Fra Giacomo under conditions which rendered its validity doubtful, expired in the arms of his favourite niece Marchesa Alfieri,

[1] Massari, 386.

[2] "History," says Lecky, "may well pronounce the Roman policy of England to have been an unworthy one, though it was both popular and successful. This question was pre-eminently one on which a great and cosmopolitan Catholic interest had to be weighed against a question of nationality, and in such a dispute the intervention of a Protestant Power seems to me to have been wholly unjustifiable." (*Democracy and Liberty*, i, 413.)

muttering the shibboleth of the moderate Liberals: " *Libera chiesa in libero stato.*" To have been deterred in the pursuit of his aims by the accepted principles of either public or private morality he would have accounted unpardonable weakness. He attacked the Pope and the King of Naples without a previous declaration of war. He persuaded his cousin, a girl of twenty-one, to become the French Emperor's mistress, in furtherance of his plans. Italian unity was for him an end which justified the vilest means. With the possible exception of Bismarck, what greater figure has appeared upon the European stage since Napoleon! Yet the edifice which the Iron Chancellor raised has fallen, while that of which the Piedmontese was the architect continues to stand.

CHAPTER II

THE END OF THE TEMPORAL POWER

THE new State was the first real Kingdom of Italy that had ever existed. There had been a so-called Kingdom of Italy in the days of the Carolingian and of the Saxon Emperors; it had extended from the Alps to the Gulf of Gaeta, but had not included the southern portion of the peninsula to which the Greeks had first given the name of Œnotria or Italy. Again, in 1805 Napoleon, at the request of a deputation from the Cisalpine Republic headed by Melzi, had assumed the title of King of Italy. The Napoleonic kingdom was, however, yet more exiguous than the mediæval one, as it embraced at first only Lombardy, Venetia, and the Trentino; though later a part of the States of the Church was added to it.

The kingdom of 1861 embraced the whole peninsula save Venice and Rome. The territory which now remained to the Pope comprised the Comarca of Rome, the Legation of Velletri, and the Delegations of Viterbo, Civita Vecchia, and Frosinone; in all, an area of about 5,000 square miles, containing a population of 700,000, as against the 16,000 square miles of territory, with a population of upwards of 3,000,000, which he had ruled in 1859. This area the Emperor of the French forbade Italy to occupy.

Neither geography, ethnology, nor language could offer any reason in favour of the continued political separation of Rome from the rest of Italy. The only objection against union was the religious one. How would it be possible to preserve the independence of the Pope if the temporal power should disappear? Yet, granted the premiss that Italy required one strong, central Government, *a fortiori* the temporal power must go. What were the wishes of the Romans themselves? Light is thrown on this matter by a confidential report made by Mgr. Lavigerie, Auditor of the Rota, afterwards Cardinal and Archbishop of Algiers, to the Minister, Thouvenel, and bearing the date December 14th, 1861. He admits that the most active and most intelligent portion of the population is in favour of a change of Government; since, should the rule of priests come to an end, many administrative posts at present closed to them would be thrown open to educated laymen. This party did not, however, number more than two or three thousand persons out of a total population of 200,000. [1]

Shortly before his death Cavour had attempted to negotiate with the Curia through

[1] Palamenghi-Crispi, *Francesco Crispi : Politica Interna* (1924), 37, 38.

Cardinal Santucci, with a view to finding a *modus vivendi* for the settlement of the Roman Question.[1] It had been proposed that the Pope should nominate Victor Emmanuel as his Vicar, and should himself retain only a nominal suzerainty over the Papal States. Negotiations were continued by his successor, the Tuscan Liberal, Bettino Ricasoli, but had proved abortive. Meanwhile Napoleon III, who after the Republican successes at the elections of 1863 was compelled to rely more and more on Catholic support, continued to interpose his veto upon the occupation of Rome, where a French garrison had been maintained ever since Oudinot had overthrown the Republic and restored the Pope in 1849.

"*Fuori i barbari,*" had cried Julius II, and the old man had donned his armour, and vowed that he would drive the French from Italy. And, as the rule of Pius IX reposed upon French bayonets, men contrasted the present days unfavourably with the times of the great Renaissance Pope. The summoning of the Austrians into the Legations by Gregory XVI, and of the French to Rome by Pius IX, proved effective weapons in the hands of the adversaries of the Papacy, at a time when the national consciousness of Italy was awakening to new life.

[1] The agents employed by Cavour during these negotiations were the Abbate Stellardi, a royal chaplain, Dr. Pantaleoni, a Roman physician, and the celebrated ex-Jesuit, Fr. Passaglia.

In September, 1864, a convention was concluded between France and Italy in virtue of which the French were to evacuate Rome so soon as Mgr. de Mérode had completed the reorganisation of the papal army ; while Italy, as a sign of her renunciation of Rome, was to choose another capital. The seat of Government was accordingly transferred from Turin to Florence in 1865. Piedmont thus lost its preeminence over the other provinces of Italy. The war of 1866 brought success to Italian arms neither by land nor sea, but the fate of Venice was decided in Bohemia ; and when Prussian arms had bestowed it upon Italy, only Rome was lacking to complete the fabric of national unity.

The establishment of the new kingdom had been accompanied by an outburst of anti-religious fanaticism throughout the peninsula, which the moderate party had been unable to control. Cardinal Riario Sforza, Archbishop of Naples, had been compelled to fly to Rome to escape arrest, because of his protest against the anti-religious excesses of the new régime. The Archbishop of Milan had not even been allowed to take possession of his see. Some other archbishops and bishops were in prison or in exile, and the number of sees rendered vacant owing to the difficulty of finding a candidate acceptable both to the Pope and the Italian Government was increasing.

Ricasoli, President of the Council for a second

time in 1866, opened up negotiations with the Pope for the filling up of the vacant sees, as a preliminary step to the settlement of the Roman Question. A deputy named Tonello, chosen for his extensive knowledge of canon law, acted as intermediary between the royal Government and the Vatican.[1] Some progress seems to have been made, but the Radical party in the Chamber rendered peace difficult. Ricasoli dissolved it in the hope of securing a Chamber more favourable to his views; but the new one proved even more anti-clerical than its predecessor. The hope of agreement vanished. So threatening did the outlook seem that at the end of 1867 the Pope told Lord Clarendon that he could see no means of averting the proclamation of a Republic save "constant and fervent prayer." The Garibaldian invasion during the autumn brought back a French garrison which remained till, in August, 1870, it was recalled to take part in the ineffectual attempt to dam the tide of German invasion which was sweeping over the eastern departments. The road to Rome was now open to the Italians, and no foreign interference was to be anticipated. Indeed, the Pope was upon the worst possible terms with the Catholic Powers. In Austria, Beust had denounced the Concordat, concluded in 1855; Bavaria was on the brink of a schism; in Belgium anti-clerical Liberalism, personified by M. Frère-Orban, was enjoying its heyday. The

[1] Cantù, *Della Indipendenza Italiana*, iii (1877), 739.

Spanish Cortes was offering the crown, vacant since the dethronement of Isabella II, to the Duke of Aosta, Victor Emmanuel's second son, while Portugal was also restive.

At Florence an Administration in which Lanza was Premier and Minister of the Interior, Visconti-Venosta Minister of Foreign Affairs, and Quintino Sella Minister of Finance, had come into office in 1869. Sella was the dominating influence in the party which desired an immediate occupation of Rome, while some of his colleagues hesitated. Victor Emmanuel, as the scion of a house noted for generations for its loyalty to the Holy See, found the idea of using violence against the Pope by no means palatable. The story is told that when Sella informed him of his readiness to assume responsibility before the Powers for the occupation of Rome, the King, deriving but cold comfort from this assurance, asked who would assume responsibility before the devil. Many of his relatives shared his scruples; but, had he hesitated to act, it seems certain that it would have cost him his throne. His son, Prince Humbert, was believed, in such an eventuality, to have been ready to accept his father's crown and to head a march upon Rome.

For the Pope there were three possible courses of action. He might submit to a peaceable occupation of his territory, making the best terms he could with the invaders. He might leave Rome. Or he might offer such resistance as would indicate that he yielded only to force, and then remain in the Vatican without recognising the new order of things. In the event of flight, the places of exile most discussed were Malta, Trent, and Innsbrück. A French cruiser, the *Orénoque*, was stationed at Civita Vecchia, to be at the disposal of the Pope should he desire to leave Rome. It remained till after the fall of Thiers, when it was withdrawn by MacMahon, and another one was stationed at Ajaccio for this purpose.

Those who favoured the alternative of flight had little belief in the stability of United Italy. Three times the Temporal Power had fallen: in 1798, in 1809, and in 1849; three times it had been restored. Might it not be so once again? By leaving Rome the Pope, so they argued, would hasten a counter-revolution. The situation was, however, in 1870 very different from what it had been on the three previous occasions. Visconti-Venosta having ascertained that no intervention was to be apprehended on the part of the Powers, the invasion began on September 11th. General Cadorna issued a proclamation from Terni which was moderate in its tone, promising to defend the spiritual independence of the Holy See. The main body of the invaders, consisting of three divisions commanded by Cadorna himself, advanced upon Rome from the north-east; while the Garibaldian, Nino Bixio, who but a few days earlier had publicly suggested that the congenial task of throwing the Cardinals into the Tiber might be assigned to him,[1] in command of the II Division, advanced across the Province of Viterbo upon Civita Vecchia. Angioletti, in command of the IX Division, entered papal territory across the old Neapolitan frontier, occupying Frosinone on the 13th and Velletri on the 16th. The papal forces, greatly inferior in numbers to the invader, retired as he advanced. The pontifical resources were, of course, quite insufficient to equip an army equal to the Italian. All that could be done was to maintain a force capable of dealing with a raid by the Garibaldini. September 20th dawned. It was a red-letter day in the annals of Revolution, for it was the anniversary of Valmy. The Pontiff ordered that resistance should cease after the breach had been made at the Porta Pia. A flood of exiles poured into it after the royal troops, and within a few hours suspended priests and unfrocked friars were selling Protestant books, while vendors of obscene prints were busily plying their trade. To many a pious Roman it must have seemed as though the reign of Antichrist had begun.

It had been intended not to occupy the Leonine City, but to leave it to the Pope in full sovereignty. The *Civitas Leonina* was in an especial sense the Papal City, as it lay outside the area enclosed by Aurelian, and had been fortified only in the ninth century by Leo IV, to protect it against a Saracen incursion. But, as

[1] Cantù, *ib.*, 802.

the rabble invaded it during the night and began to attack the pontifical troops quartered there, Cardinal Antonelli requested that it should be occupied on the 21st. This step was undoubtedly prudent, as the Leonine City would have tended to become an asylum to fugitives from the Italian police, and thus have been a chronic source of friction between the papal and Italian authorities. On the 27th the Castle of St. Angelo, a silent witness of some of the stormiest scenes in the history of the Papacy, was also given up. On October 2nd there was held the last of those plebiscites of more than dubious value of which the first had transferred Savoy and Nice to France. The annexation of the city was proclaimed a few days later, the ex-Premier, General la Marmora, being named Lieutenant-Governor. A few days later Gregorovius, returning to his apartment in Via Gregoriana, noted in his diary: "The middle ages have blown away like a tramontana."

In November an inundation of the Tiber gave the King an opportunity of paying a first and almost furtive visit to the ancient capital of the Popes. On December 5th Parliament voted the transfer of the capital from Florence to Rome by 192 votes to 18. The problem of a royal residence presented difficulties. The depleted Treasury could ill bear the expense of building a new one. Villa Albani and Palazzo Barberini were considered, and approaches were made to Vienna for the purchase of Palazzo Venezia.

The Quirinal, a former summer residence of the Pope, but unoccupied since 1850, was at length selected. A request to hand over the keys was ignored by Antonelli, and an entrance effected by force. The Pope laid the famous Capella Paolina under an interdict.[1] Early in 1871 the Prince and Princess of Piedmont took up their residence in the palace; but many of the patrician families of Rome held aloof from the new Court, whose poverty-stricken appearance in early days was noted with almost malicious satisfaction in Catholic circles.

As the Catholic Powers had viewed the occupation of Rome with profound indifference, the idea of summoning an international conference to discuss the future position of the Holy See was abandoned. The Prussian Catholics, however, for a time hoped that their Government would do something for the Pope. To achieve this object, Count Ledochowski, Archbishop of Posen and Gnesen, visited Imperial headquarters at Versailles during the autumn. Bismarck, though not unsympathetic, did not see his way to do anything; yet about the same time he spoke of the possibility of offering the Pope an asylum at Cologne or Fulda.[2] As an alternative method to a Congress, a Bill known as the "Law of Guarantees," which declared the Pope to be a sovereign and his person inviolable, was laid before Parliament. The measure promised him

[1] This interdict was removed in 1915.
[2] Busch, *Bismarck in the Franco-German War*, i, 301.

the enjoyment of the Vatican and Lateran Palaces and of the papal villa at Castel Gandolfo, and an annuity of 3,225,000 lire, the sum inscribed in the Budget of the Papal States to be devoted to the maintenance of the Holy See. Its defence was entrusted to Ruggero Bonghi, a well-known journalist and scholar. An amendment providing for the nationalisation of the pontifical museums and the Vatican Library was carried by the Chamber. The project aroused protests from France and Austria,[1] and the amendment was negatived by the Senate. A Sicilian deputy, Francesco Crispi, while agreeing that royal honours should be accorded to the Pope, objected to the clause which declared his person inviolable, arguing that he might thereby be encouraged to "conspire" against the State.[2] The Bill was eventually adopted by the Chamber, without amendment, by 185 votes against 106 in March, 1871. It became law on May 13th, and two days later was, as had been foreseen, denounced by the Pope, who, however, made no counter proposals. In November he refused the first instalment of the annuity offered to him.

Rome was declared the capital of Italy on July 1st, and upon the following day Victor Emmanuel entered the city in state. A few days earlier his aide-de-camp, General Bartolè-Viale, had called at the Vatican to convey the King's respects to the Pope, who had just

[1] Nielsen, *The Papacy in the Nineteenth Century* (1906), ii, 414.
[2] Palamenghi-Crispi, *ib.*, 73.

celebrated the twenty-fifth anniversary of his election. He had been accorded military honours and had had a long conversation with Antonelli, but on requesting an audience with the Holy Father had been informed that the Pope was too tired to receive him. On July 2nd 50,000 persons were brought into the city, mostly at the public expense, to provide an imposing demonstration for the royal entrance. Many prominent Catholics went away for the occasion, and those who remained had to decorate their houses with tricolour bunting as a protection against the mob. The King appeared upon the balcony of the Quirinal from which so many Popes had given their blessing, to receive the acclamation of the crowd, and then stole away at midnight, perhaps reluctant to sleep in the expropriated palace. On November 27th the Italian Parliament met for the first time in the new capital. The law of 1866 suppressing the religious orders and sequestrating their property was applied to Rome on June 19th, 1873. Of the proceeds of the loot derived thereby a yearly allowance of 400,000 lire was offered to the Pope for the maintenance of the foreign religious houses in Rome, but was rejected by him. On the other hand, Mancini's proposal that the Jesuits, against whom various local edicts were already in force, should be expelled from the whole of Italy was rejected by a small majority. In 1874 were held the first Parliamentary elections since Rome became the capital, and the Sacred Penitentiary issued the decree *Non Expedit* against participation in elections, approving Don Giacomo Margotti's formula, *Nè eletti, nè elettori*. There had been in its early days a small group of deputies in the Italian Parliament, among whom was the historian Cesare Cantù, which concerned itself with Catholic interests. The reasons which now led the Holy See to oppose the participation of Catholics in political life were various. Parliament was scarcely a representative body, as the franchise was very restricted. Moreover, it was difficult to expect concerted action among Catholics, since those in Central and Southern Italy were mostly sympathisers with the dispossessed rulers; while those in the north naturally regarded with gratitude a dynasty which had freed them from a foreign yoke. The oath taken by deputies also presented difficulties. Taking these facts into consideration, together with the proneness of Latin Governments to manipulate Parliamentary elections, the Holy See had but little confidence in the possibility of securing through Parliamentary channels an amelioration of the religious position.

The year 1876 was a critical one in Italian politics. The long tenure of power by the Right came to an end, when the Minghetti Government fell upon the issue of the unpopular tax upon grist. The advent to power of the Left in the person of Agostino Depretis, a notorious Freemason, was not calculated to improve the ecclesiastical situation. In Prussia the *Kulturkampf* was in full swing and Bismarck, incited to persecution by the Old Catholic leaders and by Radical professors like Rudolf Virchow, had put six members of the episcopate under lock and key. In Switzerland a similar policy was being pursued; the Nuncio and the Bishop of Geneva, Mgr. Mermillod, were expelled from the country. At Basle a "Diocesan Conference" composed largely of Protestants and freethinkers was proposing to supervise the training of students for the priesthood. At Berne the cantonal authorities, having expelled the parish priests and their assistants, had hired a gang of suspended and apostate priests, recruited from all parts of Europe, and was attempting to foist them upon the reluctant congregations.[1]

The Italian Radicals were fired with zeal to emulate these inspiring examples by initiating a *Kulturkampf* at home. Their animosity against the Holy See found vent in a crazy measure known as the "Clerical Abuses Bill," originally drafted by Senator Vigliani in 1875. In the form in which it was presented to the Chamber by the Depretis Government it provided that any priest who "abused" his ministry so as to disturb the peace of families was liable to a fine of 2,000 lire. The "peace of families" was said to be "disturbed" if the sacraments were refused for a reason not approved of by the Government. The Bill also contained clauses

[1] Manning, *The Vatican Decrees* (1875), 188.

designed to impede the circulation of papal encyclicals and bishops' pastorals and to punish priests who, by writing or preaching, encouraged disobedience to the anti-religious laws, or who married persons not civilly married. It was the most audacious attempt which had so far been made to coerce the Holy See; and its authors hoped that, if they could not humble the Pope, they might at least terrorise a section of the priesthood into provoking a schism. The Chamber approved the "Clerical Abuses Bill" by 150 votes to 100; but the Senate had sufficient sense to reject it. The fact, however, that it did so by only 102 votes to 95 was a disquieting indication of the prevalent state of feeling. Some Catholics, indeed, supposed that it would have been the lesser of two evils had the Bill become law, owing to the moral prestige which the Church would have derived from the inevitable fiasco following an attempt to put it into force. Italy has never been fertile soil for the growth of schismatic movements.

Victor Emmanuel died in the Quirinal, after a short illness, on January 9th, 1878, the fifth anniversary of the death of Napoleon III. The *Viaticum* was administered to him by his chaplain, Mgr. Anzino. Pius IX, who had sent his blessing to the dying King, had in happier days been bound by ties of friendship to the *Casa Savoia* and had been godfather to Victor Emmanuel's younger daughter, the Princess Maria Pia, the future Queen of Portugal. On learning of the King's death he is said to have exclaimed: "*E morto come un Cristiano, come un Sovrano, e come un Galantuomo.*"[1]

The King's death raised delicate dynastic questions. The traditions of the House of Savoy required that the son of Victor Emmanuel II should be styled Humbert IV.[2] Cavour in 1861 had approved of Victor Emmanuel continuing to be styled "the Second" when he became the first king of united Italy. The Sicilian Crispi, however, persuaded the new ruler to adopt the title of Humbert I to indicate that he was the King of all Italians just as much as of the Piedmontese. Another way in which this fact was brought home was by the refusal, on Crispi's advice, of the request of the municipality of Turin that the deceased King should be interred with his ancestors in the royal mausoleum of Superga. The Pantheon of Agrippa was therefore selected as his resting-place, and so it happened that the remains of the descendant of the last anti-Pope came to lie with those of Raphael and the unhappy Maria Bibbiena. It was at first desired that the royal tomb should occupy the centre of the building. To this the ecclesiastical authorities demurred on the ground that such a procedure would obscure its religious character. This objection was conceded, and the Holy See consented to the removal of a side

[1] Massari, *Vittorio Emmanuele II* (1912), 458.

[2] By a curious irony, the new King's ancestor, Humbert III, Count of Savoy, who was known as the "Saint," had been an ally of the Pope against Barbarossa.

altar to make way for the tomb. On February the 7th, twenty-nine days after the death of the King, the aged Pontiff, who had been born before Louis XVI, had lost his throne and his head, and had reigned longer than any of his predecessors, followed Italy's first King into eternity.

CHAPTER III

LEO XIII AND THE TRIPLE ALLIANCE

AT a dinner party in Paris in 1875, Ernest Renan had unburdened himself of his views on the future of the Papacy. He believed, or affected to believe, that its disappearance was imminent. On the death of Pius IX, so he averred, a fanatical Pope would be elected, who would have the support of the Jesuits; he would be driven out of Rome and the Italian Cardinals would elect a rival Pope who would come to terms with the Italian Government. As the puppet-pontiffs, who executed the bidding of the General of the Jesuits and the King of Italy respectively, hurled anathemas at each other, the Catholic Church would break up. "*Dieu nous préserve, qu'il n'aille pas en France!*" remarked the ex-student of St. Sulpice with regard to the "Jesuit" Pope. Though the author of the *Vie de Jésus* was to prove a false prophet, the changed conditions under which the Conclave of 1878 met, led, at first, all the Cardinals except eight to favour the idea of holding it away from Rome.[1] The fear of interference with the liberty of the Conclave

[1] De Cesare, *Le Conclave de Léon XIII* (1887), 159.

was so great that the question of expediting the election and of holding it *etiam praesente cadavere* was discussed. On reflection, however, the inconvenience of holding the Conclave away from Rome appeared so great that the Cardinals rejected the proposal by 32 votes to 5.[1] Manning, who was at first in favour of leaving Rome, later changed his mind.[2] It fell to Crispi, as Minister of the Interior, to ensure the freedom of the Conclave. Mgr. di Marzio, Prelate of the Segnatura, with whom he was on friendly terms, kept him supplied with information of what passed within the Vatican. He telegraphed to the Prefects throughout Italy instructing them to prohibit demonstrations against the Law of Guarantees, and implored Garibaldi not to accept an invitation to come to Rome and address an anti-papal demonstration while the Conclave was taking place.[3] At the same time, by way of putting pressure upon the Cardinals, he threatened to occupy the Vatican should they leave Rome. On February 20th, the third day of the Conclave, the Camerlengo, Cardinal Gioccahino Pecci, obtained 44 votes, three more than the number required for a valid election.[4] The new Pope appointed Cardinal Franchi as his Secretary of State. The latter, dying shortly afterwards, was succeeded by Cardinal Nina.

[1] De Cesare, *Le Conclave de Léon XIII* (1887), 164.

[2] This is De Cesare's view, but the *Tablet*, Feb. 23rd, 1878, denies that Manning wished to hold the Conclave out of Rome.

[3] Palamenghi-Crispi, 87.

[4] De Cesare, 234.

The eyes of the future Leo XIII were first opened to the light in the little Volscian town of Carpineto when the star of the Corsican was at its zenith, the temporal power was in abeyance and Rome held the honorary rank of the second city of the French Empire. As Apostolic Delegate at Benevento he had won the confidence of the inhabitants, who were terrorised by brigand bands, by causing the brigand leaders to be led in chains before their eyes. As Nuncio at the Court of Leopold I he had handled with tact the delicate situation caused by the acute phase through which the elementary education problem was passing in Belgium. As Archbishop of Perugia he had acquitted himself with credit during the troubled period of the Piedmontese annexation, maintaining courteous relations with the invaders in the most trying circumstances. His seminary had been sequestrated and he had been compelled to house his students in his own palace. He had returned to Rome only in 1877 on the death of Antonelli, with whom he had not been upon cordial terms. One is tempted to speculate whether, had he been Secretary of State instead of his rival, and had Cavour lived for another decade, the breach at the Porta Pia would have ever occurred. Sixty-seven years of age at the time of his election, he had twice seen Rome restored to the rule of the Pope. In his first Encyclical, *Inscrutabili*, he declares that he would not cease to strive, . . . that he might "be restored to the condition of things in which the design of God's wisdom had placed the Roman pontiffs." King Humbert had congratulated him upon his election, and the Pope in turn, when soon afterwards an attempt was made upon the King's life at Naples by a cook named Passanante, felicitated his rival upon his escape. The Depretis-Crispi Ministry fell on March 8th, 1878, its credit being undermined by a charge of bigamy against the Minister of the Interior. The Cairoli Ministry, which succeeded it, lasted only nine months, Depretis returning to office in December.

The Pope at first hoped to interest the Powers in the position of the Holy See. Yet when he scanned the European horizon the omens were hardly propitious. In France, the religious revival which had followed the war had been brief, and when the first elections were held under the new Republican Constitution of 1875 a Chamber was returned containing 350 Republicans against 150 Royalists and Bonapartists, and the "laicisation" of the State was speedily taken in hand; while, in Germany, a bitter conflict was still raging between the Empire and the Church. Yet, as the Pope watched, the political sky began to change. The *Dreikaiserbund*, or informal alliance of the three Emperors of Germany, Austria, and Russia, concluded in 1872, broke up through Austro-Russian rivalry in the Balkans, and in 1879 Bismarck concluded a defensive alliance with Austria, guaranteeing her support should she be attacked by Russia, whom the Berlin Congress had just deprived of the best fruits of her victory over Turkey. The recuperation of France had been more rapid than the Chancellor had anticipated, and her thirst to avenge his disannexation of the old German territory of Alsace-Lorraine, coupled with the estrangement of Germany and Russia, raised in his mind the spectre of a Franco-Russian Alliance. There was but one means of counteracting such a danger; that of securing Italian co-operation in the event of a Franco-German campaign, as Austrian co-operation was assured in the event of a Russo-German one. Though the Italian Radicals felt a more natural affinity towards Republican and anti-clerical France than towards monarchical (and officially Christian) Germany, yet the French occupation of Tunis in May, 1881, so exasperated public opinion in Italy as to drive her into the arms of Germany. A few weeks later occurred another incident which had a similar effect. At midnight, July 12th–13th, 1881, the remains of Pius IX were transferred from St. Peter's to San Lorenzo fouri la Mura. The fountains in the Piazza of St. Peter's played; the faithful illuminated their houses along the route and cast flowers upon the coffin; at the Ponte St. Angelo, however, hooliganism began and continued all the way to San Lorenzo, filth and even paving-stones being flung at the prelates who were taking part in the procession. The disorders reached their climax in Via Nazionale, where the rabble, incited to violence by the Republican deputy, Cavallotti, attempted to take possession of the coffin. The police displayed a lamentable weakness throughout, and not till the procession reached Piazza Termini were any arrests made.

The Roman riots had their repercussion in the sphere of international politics by drawing Italy within the Austro-German orbit. The possibility that Germany and Austria, with the support of France, might threaten armed intervention on behalf of the Pope could only be averted by the entrance of Italy into an alliance with the Central Powers. The Austro-German Alliance was accordingly converted into a Triple one by the adhesion of Italy in 1882. The alliance with Austria was, of course, unpopular with the Italian Irridentists, but the friendship with the powerful Government of Berlin more than compensated for it. The Vatican could now no longer look to the Central Powers for support, and was perforce compelled to look to the rival Franco-Russian combination. An incident which occurred in 1882 indicated the new orientation of Vatican policy. General Manteuffel, Governor-General of Alsace-Lorraine, alarmed by the Francophil proclivities of the Alsatian clergy, sent the celebrated jurist, Professor Geffcken, on a mission to Rome to try to induce the Pope to check them. The German agent applied for an audience, which was fixed for the Sunday morning after his arrival. Before Sunday morning came round, however, the Tsar's brother, the Grand Duke Alexis, arrived in Rome and likewise requested an audience. The Pope fixed one at the hour which had already been settled for Geffcken's, informing the Professor that his was postponed to the following day.[1]

Several years were, however, to elapse before a Franco-Russian alliance was formally concluded, and in the meantime Bismarck attempted to resuscitate the "Three Emperors' League," when, in September, 1884, the German Emperor and the Emperor of Austria were the guests of the Tsar at the Polish Castle of Skiernevice. Yet the Bulgarian crisis of 1885–1886 once more revealed the incompatibility of Russian and Austrian ambitions in South-eastern Europe, and so the new *Dreikaiserbund* was, like its predecessor, wrecked upon the shoals of Balkan diplomacy. In 1887 the Triple Alliance was renewed for the first time, and Great Britain became an informal partner in it by means of an Anglo-Italian understanding with regard to the *status quo* in the Mediterranean.

In Italy the rule of the Left continued, and the Pope received an unpleasant shock in the verdict given by the Italian Courts in 1882 in the suit brought by Martinucci, the Vatican

[1] Julien de Narfon, *Pope Leo XIII* (1899), 181.

architect, against Mgr. Theodoli, the Papal Majordomo, that causes arising in the Vatican came under their cognisance. The decision evoked a lively discussion among both Italian and foreign jurists, and even Bonghi the defender of the "Law of Guarantees" disagreed with it.[1] The Pope, as a protest, created two tribunals to adjudicate upon such causes. Further commotions were threatened upon the death of Garibaldi, which occurred during the same year. Had he been buried in Rome, as his fervent admirers wished, his funeral would have provided occasion for the most grandiose anti-Christian demonstration that the capital of Christendom had ever witnessed. Happily, the idea of interring him in the Pantheon was abandoned, and it is possible that the difficulty of holding further services there for Victor Emmanuel, had the deceased patriot, who was an avowed enemy of Christianity, been buried there, may have had something to do with this.

On the other hand, there were occurrences which gave rise to a hope that a reconciliation between the Holy See and the Italian Monarchy might be reached in a not distant future. King Humbert met the Archbishop of Naples, Cardinal Sanfelice, while courageously visiting the cholera-stricken quarters of that city during the great epidemic of 1884. In April, 1887, the uncovering of the façade of the Duomo at

[1] *Nuova Antologia*, Jan. 1st, 1883.

Florence had been the occasion of a great religious and national festival. The King and Queen had attended a *Te Deum* in the cathedral and had been received at the door by the Archbishop, who had issued a pastoral appealing for peace between Italy and the Church. On May 23rd the Pope delivered an allocution expressing a like sentiment. Meanwhile, negotiations, conducted by the celebrated Benedictine scholar and friend of Gladstone, Don Luigi Tosti, Assistant Archivist at the Vatican, who had himself been in a Bourbon prison, were begun between the Holy See and the Italian Government for the restoration of the Basilica of St. Paul to the monks, following upon the successful termination of negotiations with regard to the enlargement of the apse of St. John Lateran. Nothing further had as yet been attempted, but the prospect of a reconciliation between Italy and the Papacy filled with consternation foreign Catholics, who still continued to cherish dreams of the restoration of papal rule over Rome and a portion of the States of the Church, so little were they aware of the real state of affairs in Italy. The dreaded vision of a situation in which the popes would sink to the position of " Chaplains of the House of Savoy " haunted their imagination. France also desired a continuance of the disagreement to weaken her Mediterranean rival. Cardinal Rampolla, who had just succeeded Cardinal Jacobini as Secretary of State, issued a reassuring circular to the Nuncios to quell the rising alarm, and Tosti, who had written a pamphlet, entitled *La Conciliazione*, was compelled to sign a retractation.

On July 29th Depretis died, repulsing the priest whom his wife had summoned, and Crispi became President of the Council. He was an ambitious man, probably indifferent in religious matters, his anti-clerical zeal being largely simulated to keep in good odour with the hot-heads of his party, who no more desired reconciliation between the Church and the Monarchy than did non-Italian Catholics. Relations between the Vatican and the Italian Ministers now became increasingly strained. A law abolishing ecclesiastical tithes was declared by the Sacred Penitentiary to be null and void, and shortly afterwards Crispi dismissed the Syndic of Rome, Don Leopoldo Torlonia, when he called on the Cardinal-Vicar on the occasion of Leo XIII's sacerdotal jubilee. The King signed the decree dismissing the Syndic only with regret.[1] The esteem in which Leo XIII was held by the non-Catholic world had been indicated by the fact that when, on January 1st, 1888, he was borne into St. Peter's attended by forty Cardinals, he wore a mitre which was a gift from the German Emperor, and a ring given him by the Sultan of Turkey, while at the Mass he used a gold lavabo set given to him by the Queen of England.

[1] Castellini, *Crispi* (1915), 172.

The relations of the Vatican with France and Russia grew increasingly cordial after Rampolla became Secretary of State, and provoked some uneasiness in Germany and Austria. William I died on March 9th, 1888, and Mgr. Galimberti, Nuncio in Vienna, went to Berlin to convey the Pope's condolences to the Imperial family. Galimberti, who was an opponent of the policy of a rapprochement with France, was credited with desiring to supplant Rampolla as Secretary of State and to create a fresh orientation of Vatican policy in favour of the Triplice, in which he was a convinced believer, as he was also in a reconciliation with Italy. In Berlin he discussed the situation with Bismarck and the Grand Duke of Baden, son-in-law of the deceased Emperor, both of whom were likewise anxious to check the Francophil tendencies of Leo XIII. Bismarck declared that a restoration of Rome to the Pope would lead to a revolution in Italy and the establishment of a Republic which would enter into alliance with anti-clerical France, after which the position of the Pope would be worse than at present. Hence his safety lay in friendship with the Triple Alliance. This, however, presupposed a reconciliation with Italy, which the Grand Duke hoped could be brought about on the basis of a restoration to the Pope of the Leonine City and its connection with the sea by a thin strip of neutral territory.[1]

[1] Crispolti and Aureli, *La Politica di Leone XIII* (1912), 235 and 354.

The Nuncio, however, admitted that the French party at the Vatican had the upper hand, and he depicted in alarming colours the consequences of a situation which was threatening to make the Vatican a pawn in the Franco-Russian game. "A Franco-Russian intrigue has been set on foot," wrote Prince Hohenlohe on May 17th, "by which Spezzia was to be, or still is to be, seized by France. This would lead to war with Italy, and in the meantime we should be busied with Russia. This war between France and Italy would be extended so as to give back to the Pope a part of his temporal power. If it then came to a war of the French Republic intervening on behalf of the Pope, Austria would be unwilling to enter the field for Italy and against the Pope, and the German Catholics would also not take part in the war with enthusiasm. Russia counts on this, and France seems to agree with her. England is said to have ordered the Duke of Edinburgh to bombard Toulon in case France took Spezzia. On this the scheme seems to have gone to pieces. This news seems to have been brought to Berlin by Galimberti."[1]

On June 15th, Frederick III's reign of ninety-nine days ended, and the rulership of the most powerful monarchy in Europe devolved on a headstrong young Prince of twenty-nine. In October William II paid his first visit to Rome. No Sovereign had paid a state visit to the

[1] *Memoirs* (1906), ii, 386.

Italian capital since 1870. In 1873 Victor Emmanuel II had visited Berlin and Vienna. The German Emperor had returned his visit at Milan and the Emperor of Austria at Venice. King Humbert's visit to Vienna in 1881 had, however, not been returned owing to Leo XIII's refusal to receive the Emperor Francis Joseph should he return the visit to the Quirinal and King Humbert's unwillingness to receive him in any other city. The German Emperor being a Protestant, the Pope, however, consented to receive him, provided that he visited the Vatican before appearing at a public reception at the Quirinal. The impending visit of the young ruler to Leo XIII was a source of much anxiety to the Italian Premier, and the prospect of these august personages holding a private conversation in which the question of the Temporal Power might be broached, appeared to him intolerable. Possibly Crispi was at this time suffering from a swelled head, as he had just attained the coveted honour of the Collar of the Annunziata on the occasion of acting as Notary to the Crown at the marriage of the Duke of Aosta, though whether he recited daily fifteen Paters and Aves, as a good knight was bound to do, we may be allowed to doubt. As a warning to the Pope, he inspired an "Epistle to the Romans" summoning "patriots" to "assail the papacy in its last stronghold," which was signed by Menotti Garibaldi. Most likely also by arrangement,

Lemmi, the Grand Master of Italian Masonry, congratulated Brother Crispi on having renewed the struggle against "the Pretender of the Vatican."[1] Meanwhile, he put himself in touch with Count Herbert Bismarck, the Chancellor's son, who was to accompany the Emperor to Rome, and arranged that his conversation with the Pope should be interrupted by Prince Henry of Prussia, who was to be received in audience immediately after his brother.

William II arrived in Rome on October 11th and the following day proceeded to the Vatican from the Prussian Legation *en grande tenue*, horses and carriages being specially brought from Berlin for the purpose. A quarter of an hour after the Emperor's arrival, Prince Henry also reached the Vatican, in advance of the time scheduled for his audience, and Count Bismarck, in a loud voice, demanded of the Maestro di Camera that he should be admitted forthwith to the library where the Pope and the Emperor were conversing. Mgr. Della Volpe, somewhat taken aback by this *brusquerie*, opened the door slightly to obtain instructions from the Pope. The Pontiff, who had overheard the Count's remarks, made signs to the Maestro di Camera to close it. Had he done so at once, all would have been well, but he seems to have hesitated, and his hesitation was fatal. Count Bismarck, taking advan-

[1] Goyau, *Bismarck et l'Eglise*, IV (1913), 189.

tage of it, pushed the Prince through the half-open door and so interrupted the conversation, as Crispi had planned.[1] On the following day the Count was received in audience, and the Pope is said to have rebuked him severely for his discourtesy.

The natural resentment of Leo XIII against the Italian Premier's spiteful policy can be imagined, and a few months later the situation threatened to come to a head. On Whit-Sunday (June 9th), 1889, a statue of Giordano Bruno was unveiled in the Campo di Fiori. The event was an anti-clerical counterblast to the Pope's Jubilee, and the Pope's enemies enjoyed themselves to the full. A black banner upon which the head of a devil and the words "*Circolo Anticlericale*" were emblazoned in silver was triumphantly carried through the streets of Rome. Leo XIII was filled with indignation against the Ministers who tolerated such proceedings in the Holy City, and the military party in France had an opportunity of exploiting his anger for their own ends. The French Ambassador to the Vatican, Count Lefebvre de Béhaine, went to Paris at the end of June, and when he returned to his post, Crispi believed, probably wrongly, that he was authorised to tell the Pope that if he would leave Rome as a protest against the Bruno celebrations, France would declare war against Italy and assume responsibility for the settle-

[1] *Crispolti* and *Aureli*, 261 ff.

ment of the Roman Question.[1] Meanwhile, the Queen-Regent of Spain, at the suggestion of the Bishop of Barcelona, offered the Pope an asylum in the Balearic Islands,[2] and on June 30th a secret Consistory was held, at which the advisability of leaving Rome was discussed. The Italian General Staff hurried forward preparations for war, while Crispi sent the Deputy, Cucchi, to Germany to confer with Bismarck and instructed Catalani, the Italian Chargé d'Affaires in London, to ascertain whether Italy could count upon English support, should France declare war. He endeavoured also by means of secret agents within the Vatican to keep himself *au courant* with the Pope's plans. He dreaded a repetition of the flight to Gaeta, and would have been no more pleased had the Pope left Rome publicly. For in that case thousands of Romans of all classes might have besought him on their knees not to depart, a situation which would have created embarrassment for the Minister. In his perplexity he sought the assistance of the German Cardinal in Curia, Prince Gustav Adolph von Hohenlohe. The Cardinal called on Crispi at his private residence on July 21st. "I beg your Eminence to repeat to the Pope,"

[1] Jules Ferry wrote in 1892, "*Vous n'ôterez pas de la cervelle de beaucoup d'Italiens qui ne sont point des sots, que la France républicaine et anticléricale, la France des lois Scolaires et des décrets, nourrit le secret dessein de rétablir le pouvoir temporel du Pape.*" Chiala, *Pagine di Storia Contemporanea. La Triplice e la Duplice Alleanza* (1888–1897) (1898).

[2] Sinopoli di Giunta, *Cardinale Mariano Rampolla* (1923), 123.

said the Minister, "that he himself be careful not to bring about hostilities and to remember what his appeal to foreign arms cost Pius IX." The Cardinal expressed his opinion that the Pope would not leave Rome, but added: "He . . . is subject to fits of nervous excitement which not infrequently lead him to determinations that are imprudent." "By casting himself into the arms of France," continued Crispi, "Leo XIII has greatly benefited the Eastern Church. . . . France has allowed Russia to manage things in the East, and Russia's influence there is ever on the increase. The Pope is unaware of these events, which are concealed from him because there are many whose interest it is to hide them."

Hohenlohe had but little influence at the Vatican, whither, indeed, he rarely betook himself. He wrote, however, to request an audience, but it was refused. Thwarted in his attempt to see the Pope, the Cardinal addressed him a letter. "The Almighty," he wrote, "has allowed matters to shape themselves so that the Church will remain unable to recover the Temporal Power. . . . There is talk of a departure, and a person in the confidence of his Excellency Crispi assured me that the Minister takes the following view of the matter, that, should you decide upon that course, he will offer no opposition, and will cause you to be escorted with all the honours that are your due, but that your Holiness will never again set foot in Rome. . . . We Cardinals are in duty bound to tell the Pope the truth, and so here it is. Under the Pontificate of Pius VI, the five million *scudi* which Sixtus V had deposited at Castello were lost; nevertheless, down to the year 1839, every new Cardinal *swore* to preserve those five millions that no longer existed. Cardinal Acton alone protested against this oath in 1839, and Pope Gregory agreed that Acton's objections were justified. Now to-day the Cardinals are still called upon to take oaths it is impossible for them to maintain, and it is imperative that a remedy be found for these conditions."

Fearing lest his letter should be intercepted, Hohenlohe gave it to a certain Monsignore, who entrusted it to Pio Centra, the Pope's valet. On August 3rd the Pope sent the Piedmontese prelate, Mgr. Sallua, to tell the Cardinal that he had been much upset by his letter and would not receive him, but Hohenlohe continued to boast that he had given the Pope "a wholesome shock." Meanwhile Cucchi, who had visited Bismarck at Varzin, reported that the latter believed neither in the imminence of war nor in the Pope's departure. Out of Rome the Chancellor declared that the Pope would sink to the position of a "species of 'Shah of Persia, travelling about Europe at other people's expense.'"[1] Catalani also telegraphed reassur-

[1] *Memoirs of Francesco Crispi,* Vol. II. *The Triple Alliance* (1912), 400–415.

ingly that Lord Salisbury, who likewise disbelieved in the probability of war, would nevertheless, as a precautionary measure, reinforce the Mediterranean Fleet.[1] Austria, moreover, advised the Pope not to leave Rome unless his personal safety were endangered, a situation which could scarcely arise unless the Italian Monarchy were overthrown. The war-clouds dispersed and Armageddon tarried, in its coming, for five-and-twenty years. The Angel of Death looked at the young men of that generation and then passed them by, that he might smite their sons with his sickle.

[1] Castellini, 189.

CHAPTER IV

LATER YEARS OF LEO XIII

THE period of Crispi's first Ministry may be set down as the high-water mark of bad relations between Church and State in Italy, which find their culminating point in the Penal Code of 1889, drawn up under the auspices of Zanardelli, the Minister of Justice, an anti-clerical of an extreme type. Religious processions outside of churches, except funerals and those accompanying the Viaticum, were forbidden save with the permission of the police. (Art. 437.) Articles 182 and 183, having in view the law abolishing tithes, attempted to establish a sort of censorship of sermons, and to prevent absolution from being refused for a "political" reason; Article 184, augmented by from a sixth to a third the punishment of certain offences committed by a minister of worship; Article 104 could be interpreted as making an expression of opinion in favour of the restoration of the Temporal Power a crime equivalent to murder and punishable with solitary confinement for life.[1] To such Draconian lengths did the dread of a Catholic

[1] *Il Nuovo Codice Penale Italiano* (Naples, 1889).

reaction drive Crispi and his colleagues. The Pope denounced the code in an encyclical of October 15th, 1890, and it seemed as though the country was about to be convulsed by a religious conflict of as yet unprecedented violence, but happily its more extreme provisions were permitted to remain a dead letter.

A law was also passed secularising the *Opere Pie*, and the warfare against the Church was extended to Asia, where a subsidy hitherto granted to Italian missionaries was withdrawn. Italian schools under Masonic auspices were also opened in Turkey, but did little to enhance Italian prestige, as after a short space they became hotbeds of vice and the Turkish Government forbade its subjects to frequent them. In 1892 they were suppressed by Crispi's successor. The strained relations existing at this time between Church and State received a painful illustration when Mgr. Bonomelli, the much-esteemed Bishop of Cremona, was compelled to make a public retractation in his Cathedral of an imprudent utterance on the subject of conciliation. Crispi fell early in 1891, as the result of an adverse vote in the newly elected Chamber, and his disappearance from power, regarded doubtless with unmixed satisfaction at the Vatican, was probably not altogether regretted at the Quirinal. His successor was the Sicilian Conservative, Marchese Di Rudini, who had leapt into fame when as Mayor of Palermo his promptitude had quelled the insurrection of 1866.

The new Premier was a "white" Catholic—a liberal—and a *persona grata* at Court, but could only maintain himself in power by an alliance with the Radical Nicotera. In May he accomplished the second renewal of the Triple Alliance. One incident during the life of the Ministry may be mentioned, since inaccurate versions of it have often appeared. On October 2nd, 1891, some French pilgrims visited the Pantheon, and a man in the party who appears not to have been a *bona fide* pilgrim wrote in the visitors' book, "*Vive le Pape.*" An Italian naval officer who was in the building rushed into the street crying out that the pilgrims had spat at the tomb and had written "*Abbasso Vittorio Emmanuele,*" "*Morte a Umberto,*" in the visitors' book. Within an amazingly short space of time, so short as to make it almost certain that the "incident" was prearranged (whistles were in fact heard in various streets giving the signal for them to assemble), the hooligans of Rome had collected. Shrieks of "*Morte ai preti,*" "*Morte ai pellegrini,*" rent the air; ecclesiastics were everywhere insulted, and the pilgrims had to be escorted to the station under police protection.[1]

Rudini fell in May, 1892, and after the rule of the two Sicilians the reins of government passed back into Piedmontese hands in the person of Giovanni Giolitti. But the establishment of compromising relations between certain politicians and the managing director of the Banca

[1] *Tablet*, Oct. 10th, 17th, and 24th, 1891.

Romana, combined with its weakness in dealing with a revolutionary outbreak in Sicily, proved fatal to the life of the new Government, and Crispi returned to power in December, 1893. His ecclesiastical policy during his second Ministry was less anti-clerical than that of his first one, as he had various reasons, both domestic and public, for desiring the goodwill of the Vatican. He wished for the blessing of the Church on his union with a woman whom he had married civilly in 1878, while his daughter was marrying into the "black" aristocracy of Naples. He had, moreover, to negotiate with the Holy See for the substitution of the French Lazarists by Italian missionaries in Eritrea. In 1893 there had also broken out a dispute with regard to the nomination of Cardinal Sarto to the Patriarchate of Venice; the Italian Government claiming, as the successor of the successor of the Venetian Republic, the right of nomination. This claim was disallowed by the Holy See and Cardinal Sarto's salary was withheld. Eventually it was arranged that the Pope and the King should each nominate him upon the same day. In these negotiations Mgr. Isidoro Carini, Prefect of the Vatican Library, had acted as intermediary between Leo XIII and Crispi. Carini, who was the son of a well-known Italian General, was an intimate friend of the Minister, and the success of the negotiations touching the Patriarchate led him on to attempt a settlement of those deeper issues which Tosti had vainly hoped to solve in 1887. Of these latter negotiations Mgr. Umberto Benigni, in his article on Leo XIII in the *Catholic Encyclopedia*, writes: "It is not known on what lines they were conducted. On Crispi's part there could have been no question of ceding any territory to the Holy See. France, moreover, then irritated against Italy, because of the Triple Alliance, and fearing that any 'rapprochement' between the Vatican and the Quirinal would serve to increase her rival's prestige, interfered and forced Leo to break off the aforesaid negotiations by threatening to renew hostilities against the Church in France." When Carini died, not long afterwards, the usual rumours of poisoning were current.

On September 20th, 1895, a quarter of a century had elapsed since the occupation of Rome, and the recollection of that event was brought vividly to mind. The chief event of the day was the inauguration of the monument of Garibaldi upon the Janiculum, the highest eminence in Rome and a locality redolent of the stirring memories of '49. The King and Queen were present, though the Catholic press noted with satisfaction the absence of certain other members of the Royal Family, and Crispi delivered the inaugural address. The President of the Council, who had recently scandalised some of his admirers by invoking God in a speech at Naples, abstained from striking an anti-religious note. He quoted St. Paul and

St. John Chrysostom, and declared, indeed with truth, that the loss of the Temporal Power had helped the Pope to carry on successfully his struggle with Bismarck. For, had it existed when Pius IX denounced the May Laws, German warships would certainly have visited Civita Vecchia upon no friendly errand.[1] For their loss of an anti-papal oration upon the Janiculum, the extremists made up by a demonstration at the Porta Pia, and it was noticed that the Masonic detachment in the procession having secured precedence over the representatives of the army, the latter were compelled to form a separate procession. A similar incident had occurred not long before, when at a review of the veterans of 1848–1849, the green flag of the Freemasons was carried in front of the regimental colours, which had been brought to Rome from all parts of Italy, an insult at which the Generals in command were deeply affronted.

Six months later Crispi virtually disappeared from political life. Italy's policy of colonial expansion in Abyssinia, which had occasioned the bloody tragedy of Dogali in 1887, resulted in the more terrible one of Adowa (March 1896). The Roman populace rose in fury, when the news of General Baratieri's reverse became known, and a witness of the scene has told us how from " a sea of murderous pale faces " one

[1] Bismarck admitted as much to Minghetti when the latter was at Berlin in 1873.

mighty howl of "death to Crispi" arose and echoed through the city.[1] The Sicilian fell never to rise again. He was the most outstanding figure in Italian political life between Cavour and Mussolini.

The King entrusted General Ricotti with the formation of a new Ministry, of which Di Rudini became the head, as soon as it was formed, maintaining himself in power by means of an alliance with the Extreme Left. The nation insisted upon peace, and Italy abandoned all claim to exercise a protectorate over the Empire of the Negus. Before its conclusion, however, the Pope had despatched Mgr. Macarius, Patriarchal-Vicar of Alexandria, to intercede with Menelek on behalf of the Italian prisoners who had fallen into his hands. The section of the Press unfriendly to the Pope was, of course, unwilling to admit that humane motives had been the determining cause of his action, and accused him of conspiring to place the Italian Government in a humiliating position. The result was that the success of Mgr. Macarius's mission was prevented by an anti-clerical intrigue.[2] Had the Pope taken no steps on behalf of the prisoners, the same journals would, of course, have declared that his inaction was due to his animosity against Italy!

The closing years of the century were marked in Italy by a grave economic crisis, which

[1] Marion Crawford, *Ave Roma Immortalis* (1903), 108.
[2] Cardinal Ferrata, *Mémoires* (1920), tome III, 277–288.

culminated in the sanguinary outbreak of May 1898. The most serious disorders occurred at Milan, which was placed under martial law at a moment when by tragic irony the King was at Turin celebrating the 50th anniversary of the Constitution which his grandfather had granted to Piedmont. In the repressive measures which followed, Catholic organisations (of which there had been a considerable development during the nineties) were suppressed indiscriminately with Socialist ones, and several ecclesiastics were imprisoned, among whom was Don Davide Albertario, editor of the *Osservatore Cattolico* of Milan. There were bitter complaints that Rudini, who unlike Depretis and Crispi, was an avowed Catholic, had imprisoned more priests than any of his predecessors, and it was rumoured that Leo XIII, following the example of Pius IX in the case of Ledochowski, intended to bestow the red hat upon Don Albertario[1] who, however, was shortly afterwards amnestied. Signor Minuzzi, chief of the police in Milan, had publicly declared that the clericals had had no share in promoting the disturbances in that city, but doubtless Rudini's allies of the Left were anxious for an excuse to make war on the Catholic organisations, whose growing strength was beginning to cause them apprehension.[2]

[1] " The procedure at the military courts [i.e. those which passed sentences on these priests] was a mere travesty of justice," writes Mr. Okey (*Cambridge Modern History*, xii, 220).

[2] Many Liberals were at this time obsessed by the idea that Leo XIII was intriguing with the Republican party to bring about the

An additional reason may, however, have contributed to fan the flames of the Premier's anti-clerical zeal. In 1896 he had negotiated with the Vatican through Prince Odescalchi for the settlement of some questions connected with the marriage of the Prince of Naples; and elated with the success which had attended these discussions he was led on to hope that an accord might no less easily be reached with regard to the questions which separated Italy and the Holy See, and that so there might accrue to him a glory which Crispi had coveted in vain. One evening Rudini was received in strict incognito by Cardinal Rampolla, but speedily learnt that the difficulties in the way of such an accord were greater than he had imagined. His consequent disappointment may have inspired his measures against the Catholic organisations.[1] The Rudini Government did not long survive the May outbreak, and was succeeded by one under the Savoyard, General Pelloux. During its tenure of office occurred the Anglo-Italian intrigue, which excluded a papal representative from the Hague Conference of 1899. The pretext offered for this conduct was that the Italian Foreign Minister, Admiral Canevaro, had been slighted by Cardinal Rampolla at the *Requiem* for President Faure at San Luigi dei Francesi, though in actual fact the

overthrow of the monarchy and to establish in its place a Federal Republic, which would make him concessions of a " Temporalistic " nature.

[1] Sinopoli di Giunta, 208, 209.

Cardinal was unaware of the Admiral's presence in the church. According to Mr. Wickham Steed the Foreign Minister was personally opposed to the decision of the Cabinet.[1] The Tsar was desirous that the Pope should be represented at the Hague, and the other continental Powers seem to have been not unamenable. Anglo-Italian relations had, however, been somewhat cool during Di Rudini's second Ministry, and Lord Salisbury and Mr. Balfour deemed it prudent to purchase Italy's goodwill by supporting her opposition to the Pope's participation in the Conference.

On December 24th, 1899, Leo XIII opened the Holy Door of St. Peter's. It had been opened but once since the French Revolution, and that time by Leo XII in 1824; political troubles having rendered impossible the celebration of the Jubilee in 1800, 1850, and 1875. Though the ceremonies were now shorn of much of their former pomp, 300,000 pilgrims visited Rome during the Holy Year. Yet, as devout crowds thronged the churches, the menace of a Socialist revolution hung like a black cloud over the country. In May, 1900, Pelloux dissolved the Chamber owing to Socialist obstruction of a "Public Safety Bill," and Leo XIII was implored to modify the "*Non Expedit*" or policy of enjoining upon Catholics abstention from Parliamentary politics, at least as regards parts of Italy lying outside the former States of the

[1] *Through Thirty Years* (1924), i, 146.

Church. This policy he had applied with even greater rigour than his predecessor. He had hoped that by holding in reserve a large body of Catholic voters, he would be able to purchase the support of the Conservative elements in Italian political life, alarmed by the increasing power of the subversive parties, for his project of reacquiring for the Holy See a measure of temporal sovereignty. During the early years of his pontificate the question had been debated among Catholics whether the words "*Non Expedit*" could be etymologically regarded as equivalent to "*non licet*." At length, in 1886, the Holy Office had closed the discussion by the affirmation: "*Non expedit prohibitionem importat*." Some Catholics might still continue to go to the polls, urging precariously enough that the Pope was acting *ultra vires*, the matter being a secular one and in consequence beyond his jurisdiction; but the attitude of the Holy See was no longer in doubt. Yet Leo XIII miscalculated the efficacy of his weapon. For while he kept away from the ballot-boxes in Northern Italy a sufficient number of Catholic voters to enable the Extreme Left to become a dangerous nuisance, the "*Non Expedit*" was so widely disregarded in the central and southern portions of the peninsula that he failed to bring the Monarchy to its knees. How, some may ask, was it that the Pope, who had shown such shrewdness in other matters, should have been led to form an erroneous judgment upon this question ? Though his Encyclicals show him to have been a convinced Conservative, he was strongly opposed to the identification of religion with the cause of political reaction. In France he had striven to detach the Church from Royalist associations ; while in Spain, by standing as godfather to the infant Alfonso XIII, he had strengthened the hands of Donna Maria Cristina against the Carlists. Might he not have pursued, so it has been urged, a similarly broad-minded policy in Italy by instructing Catholics to co-operate with the Monarchy in its struggle against the forces of disorder ? In answering this question, we must remember that the long series of petty insults which Depretis, Crispi and Zanardelli had sought to heap upon him, and the attitude of the Italian gutter-press, which was ever wont to entertain its readers at the expense of "Signor Pecci," must have made it hard for the Pope to take as calm and balanced a view of the situation in Italy as elsewhere. Moreover, had the throne of Savoy deserved so well of the Church that the Holy See should be in a hurry to bolster it up ? And why, moreover, should the Pope hasten to the aid of the Pelloux Ministry, which had treated him so shabbily in the matter of the Hague Conference ? Be this as it may, by the year 1900, the failure of the "*Non Expedit*" was writ large upon the political sky. As far back as 1879, Cardinal Manning had told Mgr. Bonomelli, apparently with reference to this question, that in the existing state of the world, to ask a whole people thus peremptorily to choose between its national sentiment and its religion, was to force it to decide in favour of the former, and the event had unhappily justified his prediction.[1]

The Extreme Left, despite the fact that the "*Non Expedit*" is said to have been more disregarded than ever before, gained heavily, increasing its representation to 98 seats, and Pelloux resigned shortly after the elections, being succeeded by the President of the Senate, Signor Saracco, an octogenarian Radical. Soon after the opening of the new Parliament, the King proceeded to Monza, and as he passed through Milan on that last fatal journey, the Socialist Municipal Councillors ostentatiously absented themselves from the reception at the railway station. Modern Italy had been the mother of more than her share of those perverted human beings, who towards the close of the last century were striving by terrorism to destroy ordered government throughout the civilised world. Indeed its hero, Garibaldi, had viewed regicide with scandalous leniency, having decreed a pension to the mother of Agesilao Milano, the would-be assassin of Ferdinand II of the Two Sicilies. In three crimes which had lately shocked Europe, the murders of President Carnot, of the Spanish Premier, Canovas di Castillo, and of the Empress Elizabeth of Austria, the name of the assassin, Caserio,

[1] Gallarati Scotti, *Vita di Antonio Fogazzaro* (1920), 208.

Angiolillo, Luccheni had upon each occasion betrayed the land of his birth. King Humbert's life had long been in danger, and at length, on July 29th, the evil end was attained, when he was shot and mortally wounded by an Anarchist named Bresci, after distributing the prizes at an athletic gathering at Monza. The question of the King's obsequies gave rise to an unfortunate polemic. Victor Emmanuel II, smitten by the censures of the Church on at least three occasions, had been reconciled by Mgr. Anzino upon his deathbed. King Humbert, though never excommunicated by name, was, as his father's accomplice and heir, considered to have incurred like censures, though as he could not personally have redressed the injuries which had been done to the Church, he would not have been refused the Sacraments had he desired them. For many years, either through indifference or fear of the advanced parties, some of whose members were wont to speak of him affectionately as their "*Re Anticlericale*," he had not approached the Sacraments, yet towards the close of his life he had on more than one occasion gone out of his way to invoke publicly the name of God, and had expressed his intention to be reconciled to Him through the Sacraments before the close of the Holy Year.[1]

[1] In his personal relations to the Holy See, he seems to have been generally friendly, and during the illness of Leo XIII's brother, he caused a private telegraph wire to be laid at his own expense between the Vatican and the invalid's residence at Carpineto, that the Pope might be kept informed of the course of the malady.

Under these circumstances, the Pope, who had addressed a letter of condolence to Queen Margherita through the Princess Clothilde, and was anxious to emphasise the support of the Church for ordered government, saw no reason to oppose the King's burial with full Catholic rites. The interment, therefore, took place in the Pantheon, the Archbishop of Genoa officiating. Many Catholics had been shocked thereby, and the *Osservatore Romano,* in order to pacify them, trod on the toes of the Liberal press by declaring that full Christian burial had only been *tolerated* in the case of the late King, thereby provoking some wordy reprisals.

The new King, Victor Emmanuel III, on his first appearance before Parliament created a favourable impression in Catholic circles by publicly invoking the assistance of God and speaking in respectful terms of religion; but this was to some extent discounted by his declaration in his first proclamation that the unity of the country was summed up in the "august phrase, *Roma intangibile,*" which was regarded as a challenge to the Papal party. Labour troubles at Genoa led to Saracco's resignation in February 1901. Zanardelli now formed a Cabinet which had the support of the Extreme Left. A fire-eating anti-clerical, the new Premier would have belied his past had he allowed his term of office to go by without some measure to de-Christianise Italy. The folly of the attempts to place the Church under direct

Parliamentary control made in the "Clerical Abuses Bill" of the seventies, and in the Penal Code of '89, seems now to have been realised. Zanardelli relied, therefore, on an indirect rather than a direct assault upon the Church, and attempted to foist upon the country an unwanted Divorce Bill. The nation was deeply stirred by this attack on its religious and social traditions. All classes and creeds participated in the opposition, which took the form of monster petitions which even Jews and atheists signed. Though the Chamber contained a majority favourable to the measure, so formidable did the extra-Parliamentary opposition become, that the Ministry dared not proceed with it.

During the closing months of his life, Leo XIII had the satisfaction of receiving visits from King Edward VII and the German Emperor; the simplicity of that paid by the former being in marked contrast to the ostentatious pomp of that of the latter. The visit of the English Sovereign must have been particularly gratifying owing to the circumstance that so desirous was he to pay his respects to the Pope, that he disregarded the advice of his Ministers, who, frightened by an outburst of Protestant fanaticism, would fain have dissuaded him from it. It was, however, threatened by an obstacle from another quarter. Unlike his nephew, the English King had no diplomatic representative accredited to the Holy See, from whose residence he could proceed to the Vatican. It was contrary to all precedent to allow a monarch to visit the Vatican from an Embassy or Legation accredited to the Quirinal. However, the Pope agreed to a breach of this precedent when it was explained to him that an Embassy became a royal palace as soon as the Sovereign entered it.

The Pope's amazing vitality had enabled him to undergo an operation without an anæsthetic at the age of eighty-eight, but early in July, 1903, his health gave rise to grave anxiety, and on the 20th he succumbed to a pulmonary affection, being then in the ninety-fourth year of his age, and the twenty-sixth of that seclusion which the difficult circumstances of the time had forced upon him.[1] After a temporary interment in St. Peter's, the remains of Leo XIII were, in November, 1924, transferred secretly and by night to St. John Lateran to rest opposite those of Innocent III, which he had caused to be brought from Perugia.

[1] Many stories are current of secret excursions undertaken by Leo XIII outside the precincts of the Vatican. Of these, perhaps the least improbable is that which makes him, two days after his election, cross the Tiber in a closed carriage and disguised as a simple priest, to collect his papers at his former residence in the Palazza Falconieri (Gallenga, *The Pope and the King* (1879), ii, 337).

CHAPTER V

PIUS X AND THE BEGINNINGS OF CONCILIATION

ONCE only has it occurred that a Pope has outlived all the Cardinals who elected him. This happened in the case of Urban VIII.[1] Though Pius IX's reign exceeded that of the Barberini Pope by more than ten years, four of Gregory XVI's Cardinals were living at his death. Leo XIII's pontificate fell short of that of Pius IX by a little more than six years; yet all Pope Pius's Cardinals had predeceased his successor save only Oreglia, the Bishop of Ostia. The German Emperor is reported to have told the Archbishop of Naples, Cardinal Sanfelice, that he would make an ideal successor to Leo XIII. Death, however, snatched him away before the Pope. None who viewed the situation with open eyes believed that the successor of Leo XIII could have closed immediately the breach between Italy and the Holy See. Yet either it must be kept wide open or else made at least

[1] When the Sacred College at last consisted only of his own creations this Pope caused a medal to be struck, which he presented to each of the Cardinals and which bore the inscription: "*Non vos me eligistis, sed ego elegi vos.*"

a little narrower. Cardinal Rampolla was felt to be associated with the former policy. Since a pronounced Liberal, such as Agliardi or Capecelatro was hardly to be thought of, those who dreamed of at least a step towards conciliation spoke of Serafino Vannutelli. Italy, scrupulously faithful to her obligations, gave every facility to the meeting of the Conclave, notwithstanding the fact that a high priest of the Craft was then her chief Minister. Zanardelli, however, in accordance with his principles, telegraphed to the prefects instructing them to take no part in rejoicings over the election of a new Pope.

More than one explanation has been offered to account for the employment of the ancient weapon of the *esclusiva* by the Dual Monarchy against Rampolla, the ex-Cardinal Secretary of State. Was it the work of Austria alone, or did she act as the spokesman of the Triplice? Count Goluchowski declared that Austria alone was responsible; though Cardinal Mathieu believes that his statement must be taken *cum grano salis*.[1] Yet Marchese Filippo Crispolti is convinced that Austria's allies in no way influenced her in the matter.[2] On the other hand, Crispolto Crispolti and Guido Aureli tell us that they were assured by members of the Zanardelli Ministry that the Italian Premier attempted

[1] *Les Derniers Jours de Léon XIII et le Conclave, Revue des Deux Mondes*, March 15th, 1904, 281.

[2] *La Difesa*, Turin, Dec. 19th, 1913.

to exercise pressure upon Vienna viâ Berlin to make use of her ancient prerogative to prevent the election of the Sicilian Cardinal.[1]

At least two grievances on the part of the Emperor against Cardinal Rampolla have been alleged. When the Calvinist Premier, Baron Banffy, was introducing legislation destructive of some of the ancient privileges of the Church in Hungary, the Nuncio, Mgr. Agliardi, had delivered a speech at Budapest calling upon Catholics to oppose it. The Imperial Government had taken offence at the Nuncio's intervention, and the support which the Cardinal-Secretary of State accorded to him is said to have displeased the Emperor-King. Others connect the Austrian veto with the Mayerling tragedy, and allege that the Cardinal was strongly opposed to the concession of Christian burial to the remains of the Archduke Rudolf. The notification of the Imperial veto upon the candidature of Rampolla was entrusted to Cardinal Puzyna, Bishop of Cracow. Its promulgation caused much annoyance, which seems to have been aggravated by the circumstance, that Puzyna, in announcing it, began with the words "*Honori duco,*" in place of the traditional "*Doleo.*"[2]

It might be supposed from the indignation which the employment of the *esclusiva* aroused in 1903 that it was a custom which had long

[1] *La Politica di Leone XIII* (1912), 169.
[2] Cardinal Mathieu, *ib.*, 280.

been dead. This, however, was not the case. Austria had made use of it against Cardinal Severoli at the Conclave of Leo XII (1823), and Spain against Cardinal Giustiniani at that of Gregory XVI (1831).[1] The story is often told that in 1846 Austria would have deprived the Church of Pio Nono had not Cardinal Gaysruck arrived in Rome just too late to launch the veto of the Emperor Ferdinand against the Bishop of Imola. Widely, however, as this has been believed, De Cesare declares that a careful examination of all the documents bearing upon this Conclave has convinced him that it reposes upon no solid foundation.[2] It seems also to be beyond doubt that no power attempted to make use of the veto in 1878, despite rumours that Marshal MacMahon had entrusted to Cardinal Bonnechose the task of exercising it against one of the candidates on behalf of France. In 1903, therefore, the period which had elapsed since its use was seventy-two years. Great changes had, however, passed over the face of society during that period, and the Emperor of Austria was no longer in the eyes of the Curia a Catholic Sovereign in the sense that he once had been, owing to the laws which had deprived the Austrian State

[1] Moroni, *Dizionario di erudizione storico-ecclesiastica*, art. *Esclusiva*. At the Conclave of Pius VIII (1829) Chateaubriand is said on his own responsibility to have formulated the veto against Cardinal Albani without awaiting instructions from Paris. Nielsen, *Papacy in the Nineteenth Century*, ii. (38).

[2] *Dal Conclave di Leone XIII All " Ultimo Concistoro "* (1899), xxxvi.

of its ancient Catholic character. Nevertheless, the candidature of Rampolla, who had obtained 30 votes on the morning of August 2nd, was dropped, and the Cardinal-Patriarch of Venice obtained 50 votes on August 4th.

Giuseppe Sarto, born of humble parentage at the little Venetian town of Riese in 1835, was thus an Austrian subject up to the age of thirty-one. Save for the nine years, during which the city of Vergil was his see (1884–1893), his life had been passed in his native province, first as parish priest in various localities and later as canon and superior of the seminary of Treviso, till eventually the "Queen of the Adriatic" became his spiritual bride. One of the new Pope's first acts was the abolition of the Veto which had perhaps brought him the tiara. His choice as Secretary of State, which was not made known till October, fell outside the Sacred College, being Monsignor Rafael Merry del Val, a handsome half-Spanish, half-Irish prelate only thirty-eight years of age.

Ill-health led to Zanardelli's retirement in November, which was followed shortly afterwards by his death. Giolitti now returned to the post of President of the Council, which he had vacated almost exactly ten years before. The "Dictator" retained office more or less continuously till March, 1914, his tenure of power being interrupted only by the Fortis Ministry (March, 1905 to February, 1906), the two Sonnino Ministries (February to May, 1906, and December, 1909, to March, 1910), and by the Luzzatti Ministry (March, 1910, to March, 1911).

The year 1904 bristled with opportunities for making plain the policy of the new Pope. In July, 1903, Victor Emmanuel III was to have visited Paris, but the visit had been postponed owing to the illness of Leo XIII. It had, however, been paid in October, and the delicate question of its return by M. Loubet from almost the first moment of his election began to engage the attention of Pius X. The persistent refusal of his two predecessors to receive the heads of Catholic States while guests at the Quirinal had caused quite unreasonable irritation to public opinion in Italy, which seemed unable or unwilling to understand the duty of Catholic monarchs to defer to the wishes both of the Holy See and of their own Catholic subjects in such a matter. "The difficulties preventing Francis Joseph's return visit to Rome were not given due consideration by the Italian press and people," writes Professor Pribram, "and every alternative proposed by Vienna was stigmatised as an insult to the national honour and brusquely rejected."[1] Further difficulties had been created by a projected visit of the King of Portugal. Don Carlos had in 1895 been trapped into allowing the announcement to appear that he intended to visit his uncle at the Quirinal,

[1] *The Secret Treaties of Austria-Hungary*, 1879–1914, English edition (1921), ii, 44.

when the displeasure of the Vatican and the indignation of the Portuguese Catholics compelled him to cancel it; whereat Crispi in a fit of rage had recalled the Italian Minister from Lisbon.[1] There were some who thought that what had been refused in the case of hereditary monarchs might be conceded in that of an elected and but temporary chief of a State, and that Pius X might, without abandoning any principle, consent to receive a visit from President Loubet. Letters written by Cardinal Rampolla to Monsignor Lorenzelli[2] and to M. Nisard[3] in 1902, when the Presidential visit was already being mooted, show that Leo XIII was not prepared in this matter to make any distinction between the hereditary and the elected chief of a Catholic State;[4] and Pius X refused to depart from his predecessor's attitude. There was consternation in the ranks of the French Episcopate when the Pope's decision became known, one archbishop declaring that it would provoke a schism. M. Loubet, while willing to pay his respects at the Vatican, was not the man to defer to the papal attitude with regard to his visit to the King of Italy; since he had not dared to accompany his wife to the requiem for Leo XIII at Notre Dame from fear of incurring masonic wrath. In France

[1] Crispi, *Memoirs*, English translation, iii (1914), 225.
[2] The last Nuncio in Paris under the Concordat.
[3] French Ambassador at the Vatican.
[4] Niboyet, *L'Ambassade de France au Vatican* (1870–1904), 83–88.

much was hoped for from M. Loubet's presence in Rome. Italian friendship for Germany had been a source of estrangement between the "Latin Sisters," and though the Triple Alliance had been again renewed in 1902, it was felt that its southern partner was now no longer firmly attached to it. An opportunity now presented itself for reuniting the ties between the old Allies of 1859; while the fact that the President's visit was displeasing to the Pope rendered it peculiarly gratifying to the "advanced" parties in both countries. M. Loubet came to Rome; but the successor of Charlemagne left it without so much as visiting the spot where his predecessor had been crowned, or entering the Lateran basilica of which he was a canon.

Yet after all the year 1904 was destined to be the turning-point in the relations of the Papacy and the Italian Monarchy, and to witness the beginnings of that *rapprochement* which has continued ever since. Not long after the President had gone, the Pope inaugurated a new order by instructing its Archbishop, Cardinal Svampa, to participate in the reception of the King of Italy at Bologna, once the second city in the States of the Church, and even to sit at the same table with him. Other incidents during the year pointed in a similar direction. In September an heir to the throne was born, and an anti-clerical agitation to have him created Prince of Rome was stopped by the announcement that he would be known as Prince of Piedmont. The anti-Christian party was further displeased, when the royal infant received the name of Maria. Within a few days of this a number of freethinkers of a boisterous type assembled in Rome with a view to impressing upon the Vatican that the downfall of Christianity was imminent. Little was accomplished at their congress, which seems to have partaken of the nature of an *opéra bouffe*, save that at the suggestion of Professor Haeckel, a telegram was despatched to M. Combes congratulating him on his persecution of religion in France. It had been proposed that the Minister of Public Instruction, Signor Orlando, should open the conference when King Victor, through the President of the Council, requested that he should not do so. A further indication of the beginnings of an improvement in the relations between Church and State was that Parliament voted a small increase in the salaries of parish priests. It was also not without significance that the last Legitimist newspaper in Naples ceased publication about the same time, a step towards whose accomplishment the Archbishop, Cardinal Prisco, is said to have contributed.

The most burning question of all, however, was whether the "*Non Expedit*" would be immediately abrogated, or at least modified. Sudden changes of policy are not characteristic of the methods of the Holy See; yet all knew that the "*Non Expedit*" was but a temporary measure.

The Spanish Cardinals, Vives y Tuto and Merry del Val, were believed to be particularly averse to any immediate change, and the Pope was thought to be unwilling that Catholics should play a considerable part in political life till a more efficient Catholic press had been developed for the guidance of Catholic voters. Moreover, the activities of the "Christian Democrats," whose democratic principles were becoming more evident than their Christian ones, were beginning to cause him anxiety. After a somewhat agitated Catholic congress at Bologna in July, 1904, the *Opera dei Congressi*, or chief Catholic organisation in Italy, was dissolved. In September the country was temporarily paralysed by a revolutionary strike, attended by bloodshed in several localities. Rails were torn up to impede the movement of troops, and in Milan the flags which were flying in honour of the birth of an heir to the throne were taken down and trampled upon 'mid yells of "*Abbasso Savoia.*" Law-abiding citizens were filled with panic, and when in November the elections for the XXII Legislature were held Catholic voters flocked to the polls. It is said that the general strike forced the hand of the Vatican, and although no official announcement of a new departure of policy was made, private instructions were given to the bishops to the effect that a certain participation of Catholics in the electoral struggle was allowable. At all events, at least one avowed "clerical" was returned at the first ballots, and two more at the second.

In July, 1905, the long-expected announcement of a change of policy was made, and the "*Non Expedit*" was modified by the decree, "*Il Fermo Proposito*," authorising a limited participation of Catholics in electoral contests; that is to say, when the bishops thought such action desirable to obviate the return of a "subversive" candidate. There were, of course, murmurings; it was said that the Pope was degrading the bishops to the status of electoral agents; that Catholics would incur reprisals if the candidates favoured by them were not returned, and finally, that the judgment of the bishops was not to be trusted in the selection of candidates worthy of Catholic support. Yet despite such forebodings the decree had a noticeable effect on the political situation. In response to the limited support which Pius X was according to it, the Monarchy began to display a hitherto unwonted official recognition of religion.[1] In the spring of 1907 several incidents occurred within a few days of each other which indicated this. At Venice the King received a visit from the Patriarch, Cardinal Cavallari, with much ceremony; a warship took part in a religious function at Paola, while

[1] The religious troubles in France likewise tended to promote improved relations between the Vatican and the Quirinal, and although the French Protectorate over Catholics in the East was not abolished, certain minor conventual establishments in Turkey were placed under Italian protection.

military honours were accorded to Cardinal Lorenzelli on his taking possession of the See of Lucca. In Rome itself two minor incidents occurred which pointed in the same direction. The Catholic members of the Municipal Council, abandoning their habitual attitude, were present when the King laid the foundation-stone of the new railway station in Trastevere, and Queen Margherita visited a Catholic club in semi-state, being received by the parish priest. As the price of their improved relations with the Liberals the Catholics incurred the increased hatred of the Socialists, who were goaded to fury by these "concessions to Clericalism." During the summer a scandal which had occurred at an educational establishment in the north of Italy, kept by a pseudo-religious named Fumagalli, gave rise to an abundant crop of manufactured "clerical scandals." Attacks on priests and religious occurred with alarming frequency and continued for a considerable period. Cardinal Merry del Val was hooted while driving through Marino, and a murderous attack was made by some young anarchists on the students of the Scotch College near the bridge of Ariccia, two being seriously injured by their assailants' knives. The Pope was compelled for a time to suspend the reception of pilgrimages.

In 1908 an attempt was made by the Socialist deputies, headed by Leonida Bissolati, to suppress all religious instruction in elementary schools. Alarmed by the increasing power of the Catholics, the secret societies, realising that their influence was on the wane, hoped to turn the tide by de-Christianising the youth of the nation. Giolitti, anxious to please the Catholics without too far incurring the wrath of the Freemasons, laid before Parliament proposals to the effect that while religious instruction should form part of the normal curriculum in primary schools, it might be suppressed in areas where a majority of the municipal councillors so desired. In this latter case, however, the school buildings were to be open for religious instruction to be given out of school hours to those children whose parents wished it. The Chamber supported the Ministry by 279 votes to 129, and the measure became law. In Rome and in Milan the anti-clerical majorities on the municipal council proved not only strong enough to suppress religious instruction, but actually overrode the law by preventing such instruction from being given in the school buildings out of school-time. In Turin, on the other hand, the attempt of the Socialist members on the municipal council to banish religion from the schools was defeated.

In March, 1909, fresh elections were held; 72 colleges benefited by the discretionary powers allowed to the bishops by the decree "*Il Fermo Proposito.*" Thirty-eight "Clerical" candidates presented themselves for election, either as Catholics or as Constitutionalists; of these

22 were returned. On the other hand, the Extreme Left was represented by 109 deputies in the XXIII Legislature as against 74 in the XXII. At this stage the Pope was opposed to the formation of a Catholic group in Parliament with a definite programme, such as existed in Germany and Belgium; since the formation of such a one might provoke the formation of a definitely anti-Catholic political party.[1]

The lifetime of the new Parliament (1909–1913) witnessed an important turning-point in Italian political life, characterised by a marked decline in the power of Freemasonry and by the rise of a new Nationalism. Though the influence of "the Sect" was no longer what it had been in the days of Depretis and Crispi, yet the municipal life of Rome lay within its clutches, as was brought home to the world by an address of even more than wonted truculence, delivered by the Syndic, Ernesto Nathan, at the Porta Pia, on September 20, 1910. So widespread was the indignation aroused that it evoked a public protest in the Senate from the ex-Premier, General Pelloux, himself the artillery officer who in 1870 had given orders for the shot which made the breach.

A few days later a revolution in Portugal overturned a dynasty closely allied to that of Savoy; while the proclamation of a Republic in Spain was believed to be imminent. Such

[1] Pernot, *La Politique de Pie X* (1910), 196–204.

a situation could not fail to have repercussions in Italy by drawing Conservative forces more closely together. Yet for a moment in 1911 it seemed as though the growing friendliness of Church and State might receive a check. Half a century had passed since the formation of the Italian Kingdom, and Cavour's declaration that Rome must be its capital. Exhibitions in Rome and Turin commemorated the event, and the celebrations were crowned by the inauguration on June 4th of Sacconi's splendid monument to the "*Re Galantuomo,*" in the presence of the Royal Family and of 5,000 mayors (including one priest) from all parts of Italy. Some argued that as the event commemorated was not the taking of Rome, Pius X might have ignored the celebrations. On the ground, however, that they commemorated the resolve to take it, he refused to do this, uttered a protest against them, and declared that the doors of the Vatican would throughout the year be closed against all royal personages, of whatever creed, who should visit the Eternal City. The Powers, with the exception of England, abstained from sending royal representatives to the opening of the Exhibition.

The outbreak of war with Turkey during the autumn gave fresh impetus to the Nationalist revival. The Powers had cheated Italy out of Tunis, and there were signs that if she delayed to act, she might be cheated out of Tripoli also. The vexatious treatment accorded to Italian residents there provided the Consulta with the requisite excuse for an ultimatum to the Porte, which Mohammed V and his advisers rejected. An armada had been secretly concentrated at Syracuse, and at the end of September hostilities began. Many Catholics were caught up by the wave of Nationalist fervour and began to speak of the war as a crusade. A patriotic speech by Cardinal Vannutelli was followed by a declaration by the *Osservatore Romano* that the war was in no sense a religious one.

The decline of Masonic power now became more visible.[1] Its press was infuriated because the military Governor of Tripoli and his staff heard Mass in an official capacity on Christmas Day, 1912. This outburst was followed during the spring of 1913 by a declaration in the Senate by the Minister of War that membership in Freemasonry was incompatible with discipline in the Army and Navy. Orders were given that the speech should be communicated to all officers of both services. In the autumn the first elections based upon universal suffrage were held. This reform had been introduced by Giolitti in 1912. Though a democratic one, it had been in the past opposed by Radicals such as Luigi Settembrini, as likely to increase the influence of the Church. The elections of 1913

[1] Senator Corradini in the *National Review*, Nov., 1925, has called attention to the fact that the years 1910–1914 mark the period when the struggle against Freemasonry ceased to be a purely religious one owing to the participation of the Nationalists in it.

saw "clerical" representatives in the Chamber increased from 22 to 33. But of greater importance was the famous "Gentiloni pact" by which Count Gentiloni, the Catholic electioneering agent, had persuaded many Liberal deputies (according to his own statement 228) to promise in return for Catholic support at the polls to record their votes in the new Chamber against any proposal in favour of divorce, of the further de-Christianisation of elementary education or of fresh sequestration of ecclesiastical property. The Extreme Left was enraged at the clerical success, and when by an odd coincidence a motion in favour of divorce was rejected by a majority of 228, the announcement was greeted by derisive cheers.

So tempestuous did the Socialist agitation become, that when in March, 1914, Salandra became Giolitti's *locum tenens* the new Ministry, to indicate that it was not under clerical domination, was compelled to place upon its programme a Bill rendering civil marriage obligatory (a measure which, however, was not proceeded with).

Early in June occurred a revolutionary outbreak in the Romagna and in the Marches, "mock" republics being set up in various localities. The movement soon collapsed, and indeed seems to have been regarded by its promoters as but a sort of dress rehearsal for a more formidable attempt at revolution to be made later on. The same month, however, witnessed the downfall of the anti-clerical *bloc* on the Municipal Council of Rome, an administration composed of "clericals" and moderate Liberals taking its place. Pius X died on August 20th, 1914, the day of the German occupation of Brussels, and the anniversary of the death of Pius VII, whose pontificate, in this respect the reverse of his own, had begun during war but had ended in peace.

CHAPTER VI

BENEDICT XV: A PONTIFICATE OF TRANSITION

OF the Conclave of 1914 we have no such intimate account as that which Cardinal Mathieu has left us of the Conclave of 1903. Indeed, we shall never have one; since the legislation of Pius X imposed so rigorous an oath of secrecy as to make it impossible. Those, however, who have written about it are agreed that there existed three distinct tendencies in the Sacred College when its members were enclosed within the Vatican on the evening of August 31st. The Right, whose most conspicuous members were Cardinals Merry del Val, De Lai and Billot, desired to maintain an unbroken continuity of policy with the late pontificate, particularly as regards the suppression of Modernism. According to most accounts this group attempted to procure the election of Cardinal Serafini. The Left, which believed that an extreme anti-modernist faction had acquired a degree of influence dangerous to the health of the Church, supported the candidature of Cardinal Maffi, Archbishop of Pisa. An intermediate group was associated with Cardinal Ferrata.

The critical moment of the Conclave was the afternoon of September 2nd. Six scrutinies had yielded no result when, so it is said, the veteran Liberal, Cardinal Agliardi, mentioned the name of Della Chiesa, Archbishop of Bologna, to whom Maffi's supporters, realising that his candidature was now hopeless, transferred their votes, thus bringing about the defeat of the Right on the following morning. According to Signor Guglielmo Quadrotta, Maffi had secured 26 votes on the morning of the 2nd against the 24 given to Serafini. In the afternoon, however, though Serafini's votes numbered 27, Della Chiesa, with the aid of Maffi's former supporters, secured 25 votes, those given to Maffi falling to 4. On the morning of the 3rd, the Archbishop of Bologna obtained 39 votes, or one more than the requisite majority of two-thirds.[1]

September 3rd, 1914, was a memorable day in history ; for on it the President of the French Republic and the Council of Ministers arrived as fugitives on the banks of the Garonne, and Bordeaux became for a second time in fifty years the temporary capital of France. September 3rd was also an anniversary famous in the annals of Christian Rome ; for on that day, more than thirteen centuries before, the deacon

[1] *Il Papa, l'Italia e la Guerra* (1915), 24–27. Van den Heuvel (late Belgian Minister to the Holy See) says that Della Chiesa obtained 50 votes. *The Statesmanship of Benedict XV* (1923), 7. We know, however, that Pius X received 50 votes at the scrutiny on which he was elected, and it would have been an odd coincidence if his successor had obtained the same number.

Gregory was seized when on the point of flight, dragged to the tomb of the Apostle and there consecrated to be his successor.

Cardinal Giacomo della Chiesa, in honour of his illustrious predecessor in the see of Bologna, Prospero Lambertini, assumed the name of Benedict XV. Fifty-nine years of age at the time of his election, the new Pope differed from his three immediate predecessors in this, that while Pius IX and Leo XIII had been born in the States of the Church and Pius X in Austrian territory, he had been from the cradle a subject of the House of Savoy, having been born near Genoa of an ancient Piedmontese noble family. After serving under Rampolla as secretary to the Nunciature in Madrid, he had followed him to Rome in 1887 and had remained for sixteen years his *Sostituto*. In 1907 he had been transferred to the see of Bologna in succession to Cardinal Svampa, but the Cardinal's hat had not fallen to him till May, 1914, little more than three months before his elevation to the Supreme Pontificate. From the extreme anti-modernist reaction of the years 1907–1914 he had dissociated himself, and when in 1911 a certain Mgr. Scotton had made a vehement attack on the Cardinal-Archbishop of Milan, declaring him to be incapable of managing his arch-diocese and also unsound on the "Temporal Power," notwithstanding the fact that Mgr. Scotton made the surprising statement that he had full authority for what he said, the Archbishop of

Bologna had hastened to express his sympathy with Cardinal Ferrari. On the death, very shortly after his appointment, of his first Secretary of State, Cardinal Ferrata,[1] he chose as his successor the eminent canonist, Cardinal Pietro Gasparri. An incident which had occurred in the spring of 1913 gave the Pope an opportunity of indicating his policy towards the rulers of Italy. Giolitti had refused the *exequatur* to Mgr. Caron, Archbishop-designate of Genoa. Pius X, while not withdrawing the nomination, had declined the offer of some Genoese Catholics to subscribe the Archbishop's salary and the see had remained vacant. Benedict XV, instead of pressing the candidature of Mgr. Caron, transferred him a few months after his accession to the post of administrator-apostolic of the suburbicarian see of Albano, rendered vacant by the death of Cardinal Agliardi. Another of his actions which aroused comment was the sending of his blessing to the Italian Minister of Foreign

[1] Ferrata's sudden death a few weeks after his appointment gave occasion for the inevitable stories of poison. As he was credited with Francophil tendencies the culprits were, of course, the German Jesuits in collusion with highly placed personages within the Vatican. According to the " Abbé " Daniel " *Le Baptême de Sang,*" Cardinal Rampolla and Pius X met their deaths in the same way. Of Rampolla's death, which occurred on December 17th, 1913, Mgr. Bandrillart admits that it occurred " *dans des circonstances presque mystérieuses,*" *Benoit XV* (1920), 11. The disappearance of the Cardinal's will had provided food for the wildest speculation. The " Abbé " Daniel would have us believe that the priestly agents of the Kaiser arranged that Leo XIII's Secretary of State should be given poison gas in a tube of oxygen during an attack of *angina pectoris*, while they disposed of Cardinal Ferrata by means of some powdered glass which he took with sugar in a cup of coffee !

Affairs, Marchese di San Giuliano, on his death-bed, though the event was in reality devoid of political significance.

The approaching intervention of Italy in the European War was, however, the event which overshadowed all others. For her the *casus foederis* had not arisen in August, 1914, since the Central Empires, who were wont to treat their southern ally with the utmost contempt, went to war without consulting her. Neutrality having been decided upon, Italian statesmen saw that now, if ever, had the moment come for the settlement of the problem of the north-eastern frontier. Sydney Sonnino, who had in August advocated the intervention of Italy on the Austro-German side, became Minister of Foreign Affairs shortly after the death of San Giuliano in the autumn, and opened up negotiations with the Ballplatz with this end in view. The ethical aspects of the War had but little interest for him, and he was willing to give Germany a free hand to annex Belgium, provided that she could induce Austria to make the concessions he required, viz.: the recovery of the frontier possessed by the Napoleonic kingdom in 1811, the lower valley of the Isonzo, the neutralisation of Trieste, and the Curzola archipelago in the Adriatic.[1] To facilitate these negotiations the former Imperial Chancellor, Von Bülow, was sent as German Ambassador to Rome, much being hoped for from his matrimonial connections with the

[1] *Italian Green Book*, 84.

Italian aristocracy. But the characteristic obtuseness of the Vienna Government frustrated the efforts of the "honest broker" and drove Sonnino into the arms of the Entente, to whom an early victory seemed assured when, in the spring of 1915, the Cossacks descended with the melting Carpathian snows into the Hungarian plain. There was danger that a sudden peace might leave Italy empty-handed. Sonnino, therefore, concluded a highly advantageous treaty with the Allies on April 26th, and a week later denounced the Triple Alliance, which had been renewed for the last time in 1913, while Austria, too late, offered terms which the Italian Foreign Minister would have accepted as a basis of discussion. The military situation was, however, deceptive and soon to undergo a dramatic change; for on the very day before Italy broke with her old allies Mackensen pierced the Russian front upon the Dunajetz, and the tide of Austro-German advance did not stop till autumn, by which time Poland and Lithuania had been wrested from beneath the sceptre of the Tsar. Had the Salandra-Sonnino Ministry foreseen the course of events it would perhaps have acted differently, but it was too late; the die was cast, and on May 24th Italy declared war.

Italian participation in the struggle had been the work of two distinct groups, the Nationalists, who feared that continued neutrality would leave their country with diminished prestige when peace came, and another closely in touch

pleading for the exclusion from such a gathering of a representative of the Pope. This writer was widely held to represent the views of Baron Sonnino. A puerile article by Signor Nathan advocating a similar conclusion followed. The Hon. Soderini, Mgr. Umberto Benigni, and Marchese Filippo Crispolti then replied to the arguments adduced by these writers. The discussion was summed up in an article by Senator Valli taking the view that the Holy See might be represented at the Peace Congress, if it would give an undertaking not to raise the Roman Question thereat. The question again came into prominence when, after the second Russian revolution in November, 1917, the terms of the Pact of London were published by the Soviet authorities. It was found that Article 15 provided for the exclusion of a representative of the Holy See from the Peace Conference. Of this clause two versions appeared containing a material difference. One of these ran " France, Great Britain and Russia, pledge themselves to support Italy in not allowing the representatives of the Holy See to undertake any diplomatic steps having for their object the conclusion of peace or the settlement of questions connected with the present War." The other was worded : " France, Great Britain and Russia, undertake to support Italy in preventing the representatives of the Holy See from taking any steps whatever in the matter of the conclusion of peace, or the settlement of questions bound up with the present War."[1]

Replying to an interpellation in the Chamber by the deputy Longinotti, after the publication of the text of the treaty, the Under-Secretary for Foreign Affairs denied that there existed any clause in the treaty opposing an attempt on the part of the Holy See to bring about the conclusion of peace.[2] The possibility that it might do so, which had become a reality in August, 1917, had long been viewed with a certain amount of apprehension by the advocates of war *à outrance* in the allied countries. Though he had no sympathy with the "Knock-out blow" school Benedict XV was keenly alive to the moral aspect of the struggle. Notwithstanding the fact that the Holy See had not been a party to the Treaty of 1839, he had, in a consistorial allocution of January 22nd, 1915, condemned the violation of Belgian neutrality, a step which evoked a vigorous protest from Herr von Mühlberg, the Prussian Minister to the Vatican. He had also in a letter to the Dean of the Sacred College of May 27th of the same year, protested against Germany's methods of war at sea. He refused, however, to give his *imprimatur* to the peace programmes of the Entente Powers as a whole, and identified himself rather with that great body of moderate opinion which existed in

[1] F. Seymour Cocks, *The Secret Treaties and Understandings* (Union of Democratic Control) (1918), 40.
[2] Vercesi, *Il Vaticano, l'Italia e la Guerra* (1925), 239, 240.

all belligerent countries and was favourable to a negotiated as opposed to a dictated peace. This policy, for varying reasons, found advocates in Lord Lansdowne and Mr. Ramsay Macdonald in England, in M. Caillaux in France, in Signor Giolitti in Italy, in Herr Scheidemann in Germany, in M. Kerensky in Russia, in the Emperor Charles and Count Ottokar Czernin in Austria-Hungary, and it was one of which Mr. Wilson had been a consistent advocate till he became the tool of M. Clemenceau.

When Mgr. Baudrillart was in Rome in the autumn of 1915, he learned what were in the Pope's view the chief constitutive elements of a just and durable peace. Its basis must include (1) the maintenance by France of her territorial integrity and of her position as a first-class Power; (2) the restoration of Belgium to complete independence without any diminution of her territory; (3) the continued existence of Austria as a great Power, a condition which, however, was not to exclude certain concessions to Italy; (4) the recreation of Poland on as ample a scale as circumstances would permit; (5) the exclusion of Russia from possession of Constantinople and the Straits.[1] Nearly two years were to elapse before the Pope embodied his ideas in concrete proposals. In the spring of 1917 the downfall of Tsarism created a situation exceptionally favourable to the conclusion of a negotiated peace; and when M. Kerensky had

[1] Baudrillart, *op. cit.*, 60, 61.

suggested a peace based on the principle of "No annexations and no indemnities," the Western allies had been compelled to temporise, not feeling strong enough to reject this proposal outright. The same year also witnessed the ill-managed attempts of the Dual Monarchy to reach a separate peace with the Entente, firstly with the Empress's brother, Prince Sixte of Bourbon-Parma, acting as intermediary, and later by means of the Revertera-Armand conversations in Switzerland. The interviews of Mgr. Eugenio Pacelli, the Nuncio in Munich, with the Chancellor in Berlin and with the Emperor at Kreuznach at the end of June, together with the Reichstag Peace Resolution in July, led the Pope to consider the time opportune for an appeal to the belligerents to end the War by means of a compromise. In a note of August 1st he proposed discussion on the basis of the restoration of Belgium, the reconstitution of Poland, the liberation of Armenia, the rectification of the Franco-German and Austro-Italian frontiers in accordance with the wishes of the inhabitants, and the restoration of the German colonies. As a general principle there were to be no indemnities, "but if in certain cases special reasons existed they were to be weighed with justice and equity."

Commenting on the papal note, Ludendorf declared that it "pronounced entirely in favour of a peace without annexations or indemnities, and expected us to make considerable sacrifices while the Entente got off very cheaply."[1] It was no less unacceptable to the French and Italian Nationalists, who having reason to fear that plebiscites in Alsace-Lorraine, Istria, Dalmatia, and possibly in Trentino itself, might not turn out according to their wishes, were determined that the inhabitants of those regions should on no account be consulted as to their fate. The hands of Great Britain were, moreover, tied in the matter of the German colonies, since the Dominions could hold over her the threat to leave the Empire should they be given up. To Belgium, Austria and Russia alone could the Pope's proposals have been acceptable. But Austria had now lost her independence ; while the Western allies, in view of American intervention, felt themselves in a position to disregard Russia's sentiments. In Italy the papal note was favourably received by the Catholic and Socialist organs and by Signor Giolitti's mouthpiece, the *Stampa* of Turin, but otherwise the Liberal and Nationalist press was unfavourable to it. In the Allied countries generally the Press, with the exception of the avowedly pacifist organs, adopted a superior tone, and lectured Benedict XV on his inability to understand the exalted moral aims of the Entente. The English Catholics, whom the War had given an opportunity of proving what splendid patriots they were, were as a body deeply irritated by the Pope's proposals ; while the French ones were

[1] *My War Memories*, ii, 514, 515.

even more indignant. Each of the four Powers of the Quadruple Alliance replied individually to the suggestions of the Holy See, while on the other side replies were sent by the United States, Belgium, and Brazil. Great Britain associated herself with the American note; Italy replied indirectly by means of a speech of Baron Sonnino in the Chamber, while France made no reply at all. The replies were more or less evasive in tone and the suggestions of the Pontiff bore no fruit.

During the autumn of 1917 an Austro-German offensive against Italy was attempted upon an imposing scale. Its objective is said to have been Lyons; but though its opening moves were attended by dramatic success, it fizzled out before even reaching Venice. Upon the prospects of a moderate peace it had an unfortunate effect; for it seems not impossible that if it had not taken place, the growing unpopularity of the War in Italy might have brought back Giolitti to office during the winter of 1917–1918, an event which would have had a sobering effect upon the British and French Imperialists. It might have been supposed that owing to the identification of the Pope in the popular mind with the idea of "Peace without Victory," the armistice would have left the Vatican in a position of considerable unpopularity in Italy. The threat of a social upheaval, however, occasioned by the increased cost of living and the contagious effect of the Russian revolution, did much to obliterate the old bourgeois type of anti-clericalism. The Orlando-Sonnino Ministry fell when its Adriatic policy was found to be unrealisable. Francesco Nitti, a statesman of moderate views, who had in Paris combated the fantastic proposal to "try" the ex-Kaiser, now took office.

Pope Benedict had completely revoked the "*Non Expedit*" and a political party of a Catholic complexion known as the *Partito Popolare* was formed. In November, 1919, the XXV Legislature was elected and the new party obtained 101 seats. Its influence soon began to be visible in a return of public manifestations of the religious life of the nation. In Lent, 1920, the devotion of the Stations of the Cross was, after a lapse of half a century, revived in the Colosseum, and on Corpus Christi Day processions of the Blessed Sacrament again appeared in the more crowded thoroughfares of Rome.

What, however, was, perhaps, after the revocation of the "*Non Expedit*," the most important step in the process of the reconciliation of the Church and State in Italy, occurred when in an encyclical of May 23rd, 1920, the Pope announced the withdrawal of his opposition to the visits of the heads of Catholic states to Rome, for which a precedent had been established by a visit paid by the Prince of Monaco to the Vatican in 1916. No doubt this step was largely dictated by the general interests of European peace; but it seems also to have been not unconnected with another circumstance. The diplomatic corps accredited to the Holy See had during the pontificate of Benedict XV undergone a substantial increase. England had since 1914 maintained a mission at the Vatican, perhaps with a view to obviating the appointment of a Turkish representative there. Poland, Holland, Czecho-Slovakia, Roumania, and Yugo-Slavia had also entered into direct relations with the Holy See; while a papal nuncio had been appointed to Berne after a lapse of many years. Furthermore, the two states with whom diplomatic relations had been interrupted under Pius X now resumed them with his successor. Conversations between the Nuncio, Mgr. Ragonesi, and the Portugese Minister in Madrid in 1918, had led to a reconciliation with Portugal. It will be recalled that the breach with France had been precipitated by the refusal of Pius X to receive M. Loubet. The elections of 1919 returned a Chamber containing more than 200 practising Catholics, a thing hitherto unheard of under the Third Republic. Early in 1920 negotiations for the reappointment of a French Ambassador at the Vatican were set on foot; and, in spite of some opposition in the Senate, terminated successfully in the appointment of M. Jonnart to Rome in May, 1921, while Mgr. Bonaventura Cerretti presented his credentials at Rambouillet on August 5th. These negotiations could, however, have led to no successful conclusion had not the Pope been willing to make no further protest against a future Presidential visit to Rome. This step involved a like concession to other Catholic states.

The celebrations of the 50th anniversary of the occupation of Rome on September 20th, 1920, passed off quietly, so great had been the change which had come over public feeling. Fresh elections which were held in May, 1921, resulted in a slight increase in the number of *Popolari* in the Chamber, and during the month of June there was an animated discussion in the Press concerning the prospects of a settlement of the Roman Question, which revealed a noticeable change of attitude on the part of many Liberal organs.

Benedict XV died after a brief illness on January 22nd, 1922. His great work in the interests of humanity during the War never received in England more than a belated and partial recognition. His pontificate of not quite seven years and a half was, judged by the standard of living memory, a short one. In reality, however, it was one of almost exactly average length, since, if we reckon the number of popes as 260 and divide by that figure the number of years between A.D. 42 (the traditional date of St. Peter's arrival in Rome) and 1922, we find that the former goes into the latter not quite seven and a half times.

CHAPTER VII

PROSPECT AND RETROSPECT

IN his account of the Conclave of 1878 Gallenga writes: "The College of Cardinals, as I said, was comparatively a body of *parvenus*. There were now no Cardinals de Medici, no Farnese, or Este; no Cardinals of Guise, Lorraine or Hapsburg, to awe their colleagues with the *prestige* of Royal families from which they issued."[1] The divorce of the Church from its alliance with the kingdoms of this world had already begun. Yet in the Sacred College at the time of Leo XIII's election there were still historic names; for we find therein a Bonaparte, a Hohenlohe, a Schwartzenberg and a Howard. If, however, we look at the list of Cardinals who elected Pius XI we find that the democratisation of the Church has been carried a stage further; for though it contains names of European fame, the absence of historic family names is still more marked. Side by side with this elimination of imperial, royal, and princely names from the Sacred College we notice a wholesome diminution of the atmosphere

[1] *Op. cit.*, 297.

of political intrigue which once surrounded the election of a new Vicar of Jesus Christ and which protracted conclaves to a surprising length. That which elected Benedict XIV lasted about five months; even that which elected Gregory XVI dragged on for seven weeks. Pius IX was elected on the second day, and since his time the tradition of brief conclaves has been continued. Leo XIII was elected on the third day of his conclave, and Pius X on the fifth; Benedict XV likewise upon the third.

The Conclave of 1922 terminated on its fourth day (February 6th), when Cardinal Achille Ratti was elected upon the fourteenth scrutiny. The successful candidate is believed to have received the support of Cardinal Maffi, the protagonist of the "Italian" party in the Curia. It is thought, however, that Cardinal Merry del Val, the representative of an opposing tendency, received a sufficient number of votes to bring his election within the orbit of possibility. No non-Italian seems to have received any votes in 1878 or 1903, though in 1914 Cardinal Mercier is believed to have received the vote at least of Cardinal Amette. The election of a non-Italian in 1922 might well, however, have led to complications on the advent of *Fascismo* to power. The Spanish Cardinal in Curia is believed to have advocated the candidature of the Patriarch of Venice, Cardinal La Fontaine, a prelate of the school of Pius X, who would perhaps have continued his policy by recalling that Pontiff's old Secretary of State, Merry del Val, to the Vatican.

The successor of Benedict XV was born at Desio, a few miles north of Milan, on May 31st, 1857. Pius XI was the first Lombard Pope since Innocent XI, a member of the Comacene branch of the Odeschalchi. He thus, like Pius X, entered the world an Austrian subject; but, unlike the latter, he had no recollections of the fact, since he was but two years and a few days old when the Franco-Sardinian armies liberated the Lombard capital. His career had been a varied one. Noted in his younger years as an enthusiastic member of the Italian Alpine Club, he had later been head of the Ambrosian and Vatican libraries. In 1918 he had been sent as Apostolic Visitor to Poland, then under Austro-German occupation. In the following year he was appointed Nuncio, and held this post during the critical days of August, 1920, when the Red armies threatened the capital of the new-born state, at which time he and the Italian Minister alone among the diplomatic corps remained at their post. In 1921 he had been created Cardinal of San Martino ai Monti, and had been nominated Archbishop of Milan in succession to Cardinal Ferrari.

By giving his first blessing *Urbi et Orbi* from the outside loggia of St. Peter's, which had not been done since 1870, Pius XI assured a certain continuity with his predecessor's policy of reconciliation, of which such an act was the logical outcome. This assurance was strengthened by the retention at his post of the Cardinal Secretary of State. With regard to papal coronations, which had formerly taken place at St. John Lateran, there had since the fall of Rome been no fixed tradition. Leo XIII and Benedict XV, who had begun their pontificates in days of gloom, had been crowned in semi-privacy in the Sistine. The coronation of Pius X had taken place in St. Peter's, a precedent which was followed in the case of Pius XI. After the ceremony the benediction from the external loggia was repeated, and the good feeling now existing between the Vatican and the rulers of Italy was emphasised by the holding of the Eucharistic Congress in Rome in May, which would not have been possible before 1915.

The wave of revolutionary Socialism which had swept over the country after the War began to subside after the seizure of factories in Northern Italy by Socialist workmen in September, 1920. At the elections of May, 1921, Socialist representation in the Chamber was diminished from 156 to 120 seats. A strong Nationalist reaction, stimulated originally by what was regarded as the supineness of the Nitti Government when confronted by the Red menace, set in, and culminated in the march upon Rome in October, 1922. At first there was doubt as to *Fascismo's* attitude towards religion; for as late as 1919 Mussolini, a son of that turbulent Romagnuol province, which had been a source of such woes to the Papacy, had advocated wholesale confiscation of Church property. But the Duce soon showed that he had outgrown his Jacobin past. His policy of restoring religion to its old place in public life led to a split in the "clerical" ranks, and the Popular Party, weakened after the resignation from its secretariat of Don Sturzo in July, 1923, sustained severe losses at the polls in April, 1924, its adherents in the XXVII Legislature being reduced to 39.

Will the new régime succeed in closing the breach opened by the Nationalist revival of the last century between Italy and the Papacy? An historical retrospect, if it will not enable us to answer this question, may at least reveal its setting. The rise of Italian Nationalism created for the popes a dilemma from which an escape has not yet been found. By identifying themselves with it they would have run the risk of gravely compromising the interests of Catholicism outside of Italy; while opposition to it carried with it the danger of creating a serious cleavage between modern Italy and her traditional faith.[1]

The attitude of the unitary movement towards

[1] From one point of view it was decidedly humorous to regard Pius IX as the enemy of Italian Nationalism; since he was the most Italian of the rulers of Italy of his day. The King of Naples and the Duke of Parma were of Spanish and the Grand-Duke of Tuscany and the Duke of Modena of Austrian extraction, while in the veins of Victor Emmanuel, the descendant of Burgundian Counts, of German Emperors, and of Scottish, English and French Kings, there ran no single drop of pure Italian blood.

the Church varied in different parts of the peninsula. The rupture of relations which had occurred between Rome and Piedmont tainted it in the eyes of Catholics when the Sardinian monarchy assumed the hegemony of Italy. During the war of 1859 it is said that the clergy in Lombardy welcomed the French troops, but not the Piedmontese. In Venice, on the other hand, the Patriarch and his canons solemnly received Victor Emmanuel at the doors of Saint Mark's on the liberation of the city in 1866. In the south the revolution would have impaired its chances of success had it openly decked itself in anti-religious colours. Against the Jesuits, who were generally supposed to be identified with the unsuccessful policy of trying to make the Italian *bourgeoisie* into good Catholics by means of drastic police regulations, it breathed fire and slaughter wherever it went. Yet when dictator in Sicily, Garibaldi so far laid aside his anti-Christian principles as to confine himself to issuing decrees of expulsion against members of the Society and against the Redemptorists; while in the cathedral at Palermo he sat on a throne during High Mass clad in his red cloak and unsheathed his sword at the Gospel. Priests and friars, moreover, are said to have been conspicuous in the crowd which welcomed him in Naples, where to enlist the religious sympathies of the inhabitants he visited the shrine of Our Lady of Piedigrotta.

In the Papal States the relation of the Church

to the *Risorgimento* was, of course, more complicated. There a peculiar mixture of spiritual and temporal functions issued in a Government too paternal for the nineteenth century. An unwholesome state of affairs was the result. Minghetti could recall to what subterfuges the youths of the upper and middle classes in Bologna would, in the days of his childhood, resort to obtain the certificate that they had fulfilled the *Obligo della Pasqua*.[1] Cardinal Rivarola, when Legate in the city, required students to go to confession weekly and other citizens once a month.[2] Everyone, moreover, was compelled to eat *maigre* on Fridays. The belief even gained credence that confessors were spies of the Government and worked hand in glove with the police. Yet when Padre Ventura told Pius IX that it was essential that the *Obligo della Pasqua* should be repealed and liberty accorded to the Press, the Pontiff, though he had dispensed Jews from a compulsory attendance at Christian sermons, passed a sleepless night.[3] For to the popes much that the modern world called liberty was nought but soul-destroying licence. When the revolution overturned papal rule in Bologna the inevitable reaction followed. In 1869 it was said that every young man there would say to his fiancée: "I will not marry you if you go to church;" every

[1] *Miei Ricordi*, i (1888), 20.
[2] Madame Rattazzi, *Rattazzi et son Temps*, i (1881), 34.
[3] Purcell, *Cardinal Manning*, i, 368.

frequently, and the phrase "Independence of the Holy See" gradually took its place. "The Internationalisation" of the Guarantees began to be mooted. Such a solution has not been viewed with great favour in Italy, as appearing to compromise the national sovereignty; since it would open up the possibility of foreign intervention in Italian relations with the Pope. There remains the possibility of a direct agreement between the Holy See and Italy taking the form of a treaty between two independent sovereign powers, by which full pontifical sovereignty over the Apostolic Palaces would be recognised, and a certain enlargement of the Vatican enclave might take place. Though the Vatican stands upon soil over which Italy has never exercised effective sovereignty, and its occupants took no part in the plebiscite of October 2nd, 1870, even for such a solution as this Italian public opinion would have to be very carefully prepared. Yet as an "international" solution is looked upon unfavourably in Italy an "Italian" one might be regarded with disfavour abroad. "*Si conciliantes que soient, aujourd'hui,*" writes M. Réné Pinon, "*les dispositions du gouvernement italien, elle ne comporte pas de solution qui soit spécifiquement et uniquement italienne; à une puissance sopranationale conviennent des garanties d'ordre international. La Société des Nations pourrait avoir, pour cette œuvre de paix, son rôle à jouer.*"[1]

[1] *Revue des Deux Mondes*, Jan. 1st, 1926, 234.

Behind all these questions there looms another. Would an agreement between Italy and the Vatican generate a movement for the election of a non-Italian pope, a step pregnant with the possibility of grave complications? The Greek and Oriental popes of the early period, the German popes of the eleventh century and the French ones of the fourteenth, reigned when the sense of nationality was not yet awakened in Europe. When Cardinal Bilio suggested Manning as a possible wearer of the tiara, he replied that no foreigner could know Rome sufficiently to be pope. The Italian Cardinal objected that there had been foreign popes in the past. To which the Archbishop of Westminster replied: "But that was when Christendom was one, and all Christian persons Catholic, and Europe united, and the Latin tongue universal, and Nationalism only arising, and Catholic unity dominant over all."[1] It may be that this last issue will cause the Roman Question to remain for long an insoluble one.

[1] Purcell, *op. cit.*, ii, 551.

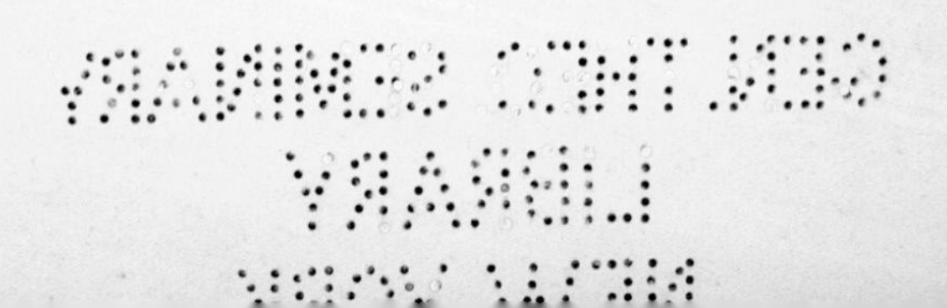